Dynamic Information Retrieval Modeling

Synthesis Lectures on Information Concepts, Retrieval, and Services

Editor
Gary Marchionini, *University of North Carolina, Chapel Hill*

Synthesis Lectures on Information Concepts, Retrieval, and Services publishes short books on topics pertaining to information science and applications of technology to information discovery, production, distribution, and management. Potential topics include: data models, indexing theory and algorithms, classification, information architecture, information economics, privacy and identity, scholarly communication, bibliometrics and webometrics, personal information management, human information behavior, digital libraries, archives and preservation, cultural informatics, information retrieval evaluation, data fusion, relevance feedback, recommendation systems, question answering, natural language processing for retrieval, text summarization, multimedia retrieval, multilingual retrieval, and exploratory search.

Dynamic Information Retrieval Modeling

Grace Hui Yang, Marc Sloan, and Jun Wang

ISBN: 978-3-031-01173-3   paperback
ISBN: 978-3-031-02301-9   ebook

DOI 10.1007/978-3-031-02301-9

A Publication in the Springer series
SYNTHESIS LECTURES ON INFORMATION CONCEPTS, RETRIEVAL, AND SERVICES

Lecture #49
Series Editor: Gary Marchionini, *University of North Carolina, Chapel Hill*
Series ISSN
Print 1947-945X   Electronic 1947-9468

Dynamic Information Retrieval Modeling

Grace Hui Yang
Georgetown University

Marc Sloan
University College London

Jun Wang
University College London

SYNTHESIS LECTURES ON INFORMATION CONCEPTS, RETRIEVAL, AND SERVICES #49

ABSTRACT

Big data and human-computer information retrieval (HCIR) are changing IR. They capture the dynamic changes in the data and dynamic interactions of users with IR systems. A dynamic system is one which changes or adapts over time or a sequence of events. Many modern IR systems and data exhibit these characteristics which are largely ignored by conventional techniques. What is missing is an ability for the model to change over time and be responsive to stimulus. Documents, relevance, users and tasks all exhibit dynamic behavior that is captured in data sets typically collected over long time spans and models need to respond to these changes. Additionally, the size of modern datasets enforces limits on the amount of learning a system can achieve. Further to this, advances in IR interface, personalization and ad display demand models that can react to users in real time and in an intelligent, contextual way.

In this book we provide a comprehensive and up-to-date introduction to Dynamic Information Retrieval Modeling, the statistical modeling of IR systems that can adapt to change. We define *dynamics*, what it means within the context of IR and highlight examples of problems where dynamics play an important role. We cover techniques ranging from classic relevance feedback to the latest applications of partially observable Markov decision processes (POMDPs) and a handful of useful algorithms and tools for solving IR problems incorporating dynamics.

The theoretical component is based around the Markov Decision Process (MDP), a mathematical framework taken from the field of Artificial Intelligence (AI) that enables us to construct models that change according to sequential inputs. We define the framework and the algorithms commonly used to optimize over it and generalize it to the case where the inputs aren't reliable. We explore the topic of reinforcement learning more broadly and introduce another tool known as a Multi-Armed Bandit which is useful for cases where exploring model parameters is beneficial. Following this we introduce theories and algorithms which can be used to incorporate dynamics into an IR model before presenting an array of state-of-the-art research that already does, such as in the areas of session search and online advertising.

Change is at the heart of modern Information Retrieval systems and this book will help equip the reader with the tools and knowledge needed to understand *Dynamic Information Retrieval Modeling*.

KEYWORDS

dynamic information retrieval, information retrieval models, reinforcement learning, Markov decision process, recommender systems, information retrieval, information retrieval evaluation

Grace: To my loved ones

Marc: To Sarah

Jun: To my son Tintin

Contents

Acknowledgments

The authors would like to thank Dr. Xuchu Dong for his assistance with the book and Xiaoxue Zhao and Weinan Zhang for their assistance with Chapter 5.

The authors would also like to give acknowledgment to Professor Charlie Clarke, Professor Maarten de Rijke, and Dr. Emine Yilmaz for their insight and discussions on the topic of Dynamic Information Retrieval Modeling. We would also like to thank all at Morgan & Claypool and in particular Diane Cerra for her help throughout the production of this book.

The research is supported by DARPA FA8750-14-2-0226, NSF IIS-1453721, and NSF CNS-1223825. The discussions in this book are entirely based on published research, publicly available datasets and the authors' own judgments rather than on the internal practice of any organization. All content represents the opinion of the authors, which is not necessarily shared or endorsed by their respective employers and/or sponsors.

Grace Hui Yang, Marc Sloan, and Jun Wang
May 2016

CHAPTER 1

Introduction

We shall attempt to define intelligence, as have others before us, as *"goal-directed adaptive behavior."*

Robert J. Sternberg
Handbook of Human Intelligence (1982, pg. 3)

The **Information Retrieval (IR)** ecosystem is a dynamic one: users translate their information needs into an assortment of meaningful interactions with IR systems; corpora and search logs follow behind the slowly shifting world they are gathered from; language, interpretation, and intent all change with time.

Change is at the heart of a modern information retrieval system. Search tasks are complex and often exploratory, with the user broadcasting signals of search intent over multiple stages of retrieval, specializing or generalizing their information needs over time [253]. Further to this, advances in IR interface, personalization and ad display demand models that can react to users in real time and in an intelligent, contextual way. Examples include query reformulation in session search [229], item ratings in collaborative filtering [111] and maximizing revenue generated from web advertisements [269]. The aim of dynamic information retrieval modeling is to find IR solutions that are responsive to a changing environment, that learn from past interactions and that predict future utility.

1.1 DYNAMICS IN INFORMATION RETRIEVAL

Information retrieval has been a topic of research for over half a century, and dynamics has been a subtopic in engineering for twice as long; why is it that now we are increasingly seeing the merging of the two? Here we consider this question by making use of the session search example in Table 1.1, a sequence of queries issued by a single user in pursuit of satisfying an information need.

The complexity of the queries in this example is indicative of the dynamics that naturally occur in modern search systems. Session search neatly encapsulates the properties of Dynamic IR as it occurs over a series of distinct stages each dependent on the last (the query reformulations), captures rich user information (clicks, reformulation changes, dwell time, etc.) and usually ends when the user's information need has been satisfied or the user abandons the search [74]. The example in Table 1.1 demonstrates all of these properties. In this case, searching over a single topic gives rise to a large number of queries which can be grouped into distinct subtopics falling

Table 1.1: Session 87 from the TREC 2013 Session Track dataset [132], the topic is: "*Suppose you're planning a trip to the United States. You will be there for a month and able to travel within a 150-mile radius of your destination. With that constraint, what are the best cities to consider as possible destinations?*" A * indicates instances where a map vertical could have been used. The query *Type* was heuristically assigned by the authors and follows the taxonomy outlined by Broder [31]. Differences in shading indicate inferred change in the subtopic search intent of the information need.

#	Query	Clicks (dwell time)	Type
1	best us destinations	1 (126.9s)	Explorative
2	distance new york boston	0	Informational
3	maps.bing.com*	0	Navigational
4	maps*	0	Navigational
5	bing maps*	1 (87.9s)	Navigational
6	hartford tourism	1 (38.3s)	Explorative
7	bing maps*	1 (5.9s)	Navigational
8	hartford visitors	1 (42.2s)	Explorative
9	hartford connecticut tourism	3 (147.8s)	Informational
10	hartford boston travel	1 (106.2s)	Informational
11	boston tourism	1 (29.6s)	Explorative
12	nyc tourism	1 (26.7s)	Explorative
13	philadelphia nyc distance	0	Informational
14	bing maps*	1 (39.7s)	Navigational
15	philadelphia washington dc distance	0	Informational
16	bing maps*	1 (39.2s)	Navigational
17	philadelphia tourism	1 (12.3s)	Explorative
18	washing dc tourism	1 (26.5s)	Explorative
19	philadelphia nyc travel	0	Informational
20	philadelphia nyc train	0	Informational
21	philadelphia nyc bus	0	Informational

into various search type classifications, illustrated in the example in Table 1.1. As the user interacts with individual search results their information need is affected by the snippets, documents and other information they encounter (as described in the interactive search literature [203]). These interactions can affect the next query in the session [229], leading to further interactions and the evolution of the user's information need.

Another motivating information retrieval application is the dynamics presented in the recommender systems. Figure 1.1 shows an example of dynamics in music recommender systems. Here, the music service is able to explore different song choices and respond to the user's feedback, whether explicitly through use of the "like" or "dislike" buttons, or implicitly through observing clicks of the "next song" button. Through these interactions, the service improves and plays music "relevant" to the user. In this case, the service is required to constantly learn a user's interests from the feedback and at the same time a user's interest can change and even be discovered over time when new songs are fed into the system.

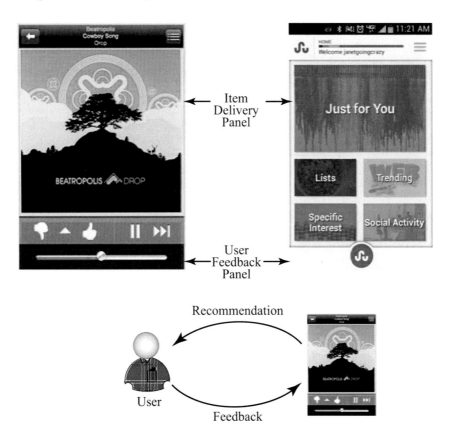

Figure 1.1: Example interactions in recommender systems, in this case the Pandora music recommendation app and the StumbleUpon website discovery service. Users of both services receive recommended content and can optionally give feedback, resulting in an ongoing recommendation-feedback loop.

Typically, IR systems can be broken down into broadly five elements, the *user*, their *information needs* and the *queries* that they use to represent them, the *documents* being retrieved and

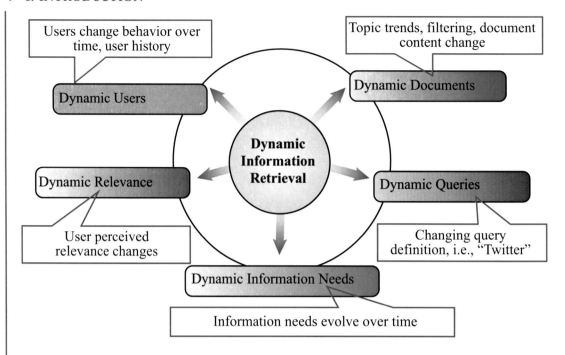

Figure 1.2: Dynamics in information retrieval systems.

their underlying *relevance* to the queries. Each of these components can be considered as a dynamic element depending on the IR problem being addressed. Figure 1.2 shows our view of the elements in the dynamic information retrieval ecosystem.

Users   A single user can be considered as a dynamic agent in the case where their context or descriptive features may change over time. For instance, during a session search the user's contextual search preference can be updated based on their observed actions [224]; their physical location [41] or their search history can be used to personalize search results and identify when they are behaving atypically [79]. A population of users may also be considered dynamic, with each different user a new signal in the system. This is the case with online learning to rank and is explored further in Chapter 3. The former case is less explored in IR research; much of the existing work focuses on learning and using features for a particular user and doesn't allow for them to change, although [79] recently investigated how to detect when a user was exhibiting atypical behavior. For the latter, the system needs to adapt to different users' needs or at least cater to the general population made up of users exhibiting different search behavior such as in online learning to rank [107].

Information Needs   An information need may dynamically evolve over the course of an exploratory search session [2]. A user may also have several information needs that are satisfied over their interactions with the search system [235]. Search results diversification is one method for addressing a dynamic or complex information need and there has been some research into learning diverse rankings of documents over time based on user clicks [189]. Given that information needs are difficult to define and categorize, one can also consider research which attempts to learn information needs over a period of time by using an online clustering technique and identifying trends and modeling topic popularity [185].

Queries   For a fixed information need in session search, a user will issue multiple queries, such as in Table 1.1. Understanding the dynamics of queries in session search is the subject of Chapter 4. The queries that users use for the same information need may change over time depending on the evolution of the language used to describe the need, or the definition of the need itself [146]. By observing these trends in search logs, query suggestion agents can be built that can also take into account user attributes such as gender or age [40, 223].

Documents   The content of individual documents can be considered dynamic. For instance, the content of some webpages (such as Wikipedia[1] articles) has been found to meaningfully change over time [1, 82]. In addition to this, the language used in a document may have changed since the document's creation, with certain terms having a different interpretation nowadays to that originally intended [176]. Collections of documents may also dynamically change over time, for instance, adaptive filtering is used when retrieval occurs over a stream of documents [98], and the available documents in a corpus decreases during interactive retrieval when feedback is gained on already displayed documents. This is also the case with the multi-page search scenario covered in Chapter 3.

Relevance   Dynamically changing relevance reflects the dynamics of the world. For instance, a news event such as a natural disaster or the death of a notable person may render documents that were previously relevant as irrelevant and result in different or new documents becoming relevant [154, 263]. Further to this, natural language is dynamic; new words, phrases, colloquialisms, brand names and products change the meanings of queries and terms, resulting in a change to the relevance of documents. For example, users searching for the query `twitter` a decade ago may have been interested in birdsong, whereas now they are more likely to be entering a navigational query to access the popular microblogging website[2] [76].

1.2   CHALLENGES

The challenge of incorporating these dynamic elements into IR demands that search systems upgrade themselves from performing simple retrieval tasks to becoming decision engines that can

---

[1]http://wikipedia.org/
[2]http://twitter.com/

pick the best choice for information seeking dynamic tasks. Search systems are evolving into natural language, conversational question answering services that need to be able to update relevance based on previous interactions and context [101]. As the world wide web ages the content of web pages changes, queries change meaning, information needs become redefined and user characteristics change.

In conventional IR, probabilistic modeling has largely been confined to what can be defined as *static* problems, where a set of parameters for a model are learned from a dataset and fixed for use in an IR system. Examples include adhoc ranking and retrieval relevance scoring such as the BM25 model [196], topic modeling using latent dirichlet allocation [252] or learning to rank [163]. Underlying the solutions to these problems are static frameworks such as the classic probability ranking principle [198] which justifies the simplest and most powerful ranking rule in IR: ranking documents in decreasing order of their probability of relevance. The described models are not capable of representing search tasks that operate over multiple stages nor can they incorporate user feedback.

1.3   OVERVIEW OF DYNAMIC IR

Dynamic Information Retrieval (Dynamic IR) modeling is way of understanding IR systems within this ecosystem. Dynamic elements are evident in many existing IR systems and data collections, yet are not fully exploited by conventional IR methods.

In dynamic information retrieval modeling, information seeking is considered from a more comprehensive perspective: the user and the search system interact and work together in a complex way to realize a mutual goal, to satisfy the user's information need. This need may evolve and only become defined while the search progresses. Nonetheless, the user and the search engine explore the information space in tandem in order to realize it. The stages of a session search are a dialog, whereby the user communicates their intentions through their query and the search system responds with relevant documents. Through feedback and interaction with the search interface the user also broadcasts their preferences. In a dynamic search system, the goal ultimately is to satisfy the user over the whole search session, not just for a single query. It achieves this by dynamically learning from the user and adjusting to their actions.

For several decades, information seeking has been an important field of research in Information Science (IS) and IR. It concerns the broad range of interactions that a user goes through when using an actual search system in order to satisfy an information need. The field came about as a reaction to the Cranfield evaluation methodology's [63] inability to accurately corroborate user studies [105]. Under Cranfield, users are assumed to search for single queries representing their information need, read search results from top to bottom and recognize relevant results when found. Thus, typically used metrics such as precision, recall and average precision measured using binary relevance judgments are sufficient for comparing the effectiveness of ranking and retrieval algorithms.

Over the years objections have been raised concerning the suitability of this framework for evaluating real search systems [136]. A broad range of research has shown that the process of information seeking is complex, with users exhibiting a number of behaviors that are influenced by different factors [203]. A small selection of factors that can influence a typical search include: the type of search (navigational, explorative etc.) [31], the difficulty in choosing a query [43], snippets and titles [174], advertisements and the quality of webpages. During a search, the user encounters a number of different information sources which can cause changes in their information need or even satisfy their need without visiting any webpages. In recognition of this, for a number of years the **Text REtrieval Conference (TREC)**[3] organized an interactive track in order to stimulate discussion on building and evaluating search systems based on realistic user assumptions [104].

TREC is the annual evaluation of IR systems conducted at the National Institute of Science and Technology (NIST) since 1992. "The TREC conferences encourage research within the information retrieval community by providing the infrastructure necessary for large-scale evaluation of text retrieval methodologies."[4] Tasks that involved multiple runs of search iterations have been studied multiple times in TREC. From 1997 to 2002, the TREC Interactive Track [147, 181] investigated interactive, session-based search tasks with a human user in the loop. From 2010 to 2014, the TREC Session Track [131–133] sought to evaluate search effectiveness for the last iteration of retrieval at the end of a session given query logs of all previous iterations. The Session Track used an effectiveness measure for ad-hoc retrieval, nDCG [113], as the main metric to only evaluate the last iteration. Since 2015, the TREC Dynamic Domain (DD) Track [260] has revamped the interest of session-based search, by providing a real-time simulated user (called the "jig") interacting with a search system for a number of iterations until the search stops. In this book, we will use a few related TREC Tracks and datasets to illustrate the principles and effectiveness of the Dynamic IR models. We will also discuss how to evaluate dynamic IR systems in Chapter 6.

It is the user's interactive strategies with the search system that are considered in the traditional definition of interactive IR. In this book, we instead consider interactivity from the system's viewpoint. The complexity of user interactions investigated in traditional information seeking research drives the need for dynamic IR. The recognition that a search system will not always satisfy the user's information need after a single query, or that the user will be unable to accurately define their need, or that their need will change over time, requires the search system to accommodate multiple states of search. A dynamic search system can capitalize on this by being responsive to the user at each state.

In this book, we look at the problem from a novel perspective. The term *"dynamics"* is taken from physics to describe systems that manipulate the Newtonian laws of motion, for example, by altering the velocity of a pendulum using damping forces [180]. Control theory, a related subfield, is the mathematics of closed feedback looping systems that maintain some form of equilibrium

---

[3]http://trec.nist.gov/
[4]http://trec.nist.gov

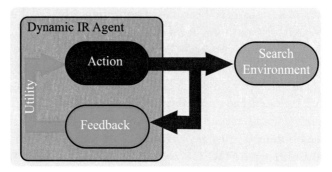

Figure 1.3: The closed feedback loop of a dynamic agent in IR. The agent senses its search environment using its feedback sensor and converts this into a utility value. This value determines the action that the agent takes, which affects the external environment, and the process repeats.

or **state**, for instance, a pendulum that continuously oscillates due to the repeated application of some force [75]. Such systems are described as dynamic **agents**, comprised of a **feedback** sensor that measures some aspect of the environment, which is used by the agent to determine an **action** that affects the environment. A dynamic agent for IR is depicted in Figure 1.3.

Agents exhibit *goal-directed adaptive behavior*, a phrase used by Robert J. Sternberg to describe human intelligence [237]. While he also merits memory, reasoning and abstraction amongst other definitive traits, nonetheless one can label a dynamic agent an intelligent one, responsive to the dynamics of its real world setting so that it can achieve its goal. Dynamic agents are resistant to adverse change or error and are able to learn and adapt to their surroundings. Many agents maintain a model of their environment so that they can understand how it will react given some input into it.

More generally, a Dynamic IR modeling system is one which exhibits the following three defining characteristics:

Rich Interactions A dynamic system is one which can sense its environment so that it may respond to it and affect it. In order for a Dynamic IR system to be adaptive it must be able to determine what state it resides in, whether this is the state of the user, the system or any other representation of the IR process. The interaction may take many forms depending on the system and the problem being solved, typical examples include user feedback (explicit and implicit), query reformulations, eye and mouse movements and so on. The interaction is the signal received by the Dynamic IR system so that it may formulate its next action.

Temporal Dependency A dynamic system must operate across multiple distinct phases or time steps, otherwise a simple static system would suffice. The purpose of detecting a rich interaction is so that the Dynamic IR system can respond accordingly in a way that is dependent on the previous interaction(s). The response can manifest itself in different ways depending on the IR problem, for instance, the ads shown to a user may change depending on items added to a basket on an e-commerce website, or search results re-ranked according to click-throughs. The actions available are usually those which the system is capable of in a static setting, but with temporal dependency the system can choose different actions at different stages. The temporal dependency indicates the presence of the Markov property which is explored in more detail in Chapter 4.

Overall Goal A dynamic system targets an over-arching goal. This goal affects the actions taken at every stage and may cause the system to perform sub-optimally at a particular stage in order to gain greater rewards elsewhere. Defining and optimizing this goal remains a key challenge in the setting up of a Dynamic IR model. The interaction signal can be used to interpret the proximity to the goal or a distinct reward may be observable instead. Abstract examples of goals across multiple stages in IR include user satisfaction, ROI maximization or improving the system's overall performance.

In this book, the difference between dynamic and traditional IR is explored; the elements that constitute a framework for general Dynamic IR systems are identified and then related to research in current areas of academic interest in IR. Along the way, key characteristics of Dynamic IR such as diversity and exploration are covered in more detail.

1.4   AIMS OF THIS BOOK

Dynamic information retrieval is an emerging subtopic in the field of IR. The objective of this book is to provide a comprehensive and up-to-date introduction to the field of dynamic information retrieval. This is achieved by defining a framework for Dynamic IR as a natural progression in IR research complexity: where early research concerned *static* problems such as adhoc retrieval, which gave way to *interactive* tasks such as those incorporating relevance feedback [201], which has led to *dynamic* systems for tasks such as session search ranking [167]. This framework incorporates dynamic elements common to Dynamic IR systems, and these are explored through some of its various applications: session search, online learning to rank, recommender systems and evaluation. Our survey of this literature expands upon areas in reinforcement learning and artificial intelligence pertinent to Dynamic IR such as Markov Decision processes and multi-armed bandit theory.

This book is a natural follow-up to previous statistical IR modeling surveys and is relevant to researchers working in the areas of statistical modeling, personalization and recommendation, and practitioners in Web search, online advertising and big data. This book is intended for people interested in information retrieval and machine learning who wish to understand how IR is changing. Through this book, readers will gain a deeper understanding of the dynamics in IR systems and how they can be modeled using modern IR and reinforcement learning techniques. Suggested pre-requisites to the material in this book include a familiarity with probabilistic graphical modeling, a good background in information retrieval and a general understanding of machine learning.

1.5   STRUCTURE

In the first half of this book, we focus on establishing the Dynamic IR framework. In Chapter 2 Dynamic IR is framed in the context of historical advances in the field. We compare the areas of static, interactive and Dynamic IR and through their differences identify the key components that define a Dynamic IR problem.

The remainder of the book is application-led, with each chapter summarizing a different practical use of Dynamic IR and showcasing statistical techniques that are effective within that area. For instance, Chapter 3 extends dynamic search to multiple users by focusing on adaptive filtering and online learning to rank. Here, we explore the multi-armed bandit theory and the balance of exploration and exploitation in Dynamic IR. The focus in Chapter 4 is session search, an area of IR research that lends itself naturally to Dynamic IR. In this chapter we go over partially observable Markov decision processes and show how they can help improve dynamic session search. We shift the focus onto recommender systems in Chapter 5 and the evaluation of dynamic systems in Chapter 6. Finally, we summarize the book in Chapter 7 and outline open areas of research in dynamic information retrieval modeling.

CHAPTER 2

Information Retrieval Frameworks

Before we start identifying specific areas of IR research that can be described using the dynamic IR models that we present in this book, we take a more general view of problems in IR by representing them conceptually, distinguishing between static, interactive and dynamic models. For instance, with regard to ranking and retrieval, a static model is one where no user feedback is considered, an interactive model incorporates feedback but only to immediately improve the ranking, and a dynamic model uses feedback to optimize and plan for every user interaction. Each of the framework categories are a generalization of the previous. Similar trends are observed in other areas of IR research, for example the early term-based vector space retrieval model gave way to more complex models like BM25 [196] and language modeling [187]. Likewise, the evolution from static to interactive and then dynamic IR reflects the increasing complexity of search problems and the need for responsive solutions. In this chapter, each conceptual model is presented along with an associated framework for solving IR problems in that model, and a case study example application of the framework.

In this chapter, we use multi-page search as an example problem in Information Retrieval to demonstrate the different treatments of static, interactive and dynamic information retrieval. Multi-page search concerns the ranking of documents over multiple pages of search results where documents are retrieved for a single query, ranked and then segregated into pages of documents. On each page, a user may examine and click on documents and the goal is to use this feedback to improve the rankings over any remaining pages of search.

2.1 CASE STUDY: MULTI-PAGE SEARCH

The **Multi-Page Search (MPS)** scenario concerns the ranking of documents over multiple pages of search results [120, 139]. MPS typically models exploratory search queries which are more likely to lead to multi-query sessions and multi-page searches [253] (with one study finding that 27% of such searches occur over multiple pages [112]). In this scenario documents are retrieved for a single query, ranked and then segregated into pages of M documents. On each page, a user may examine and click on documents. We assume that the user will return to the results page and move onto the next page and we define a threshold of T pages which the user will search over. The goal in MPS is to create rankings of relevant documents across T pages. For the pages following the first, document clicks can be used to personalize search rankings.

The multi-page search problem is familiar and easily definable in static, interactive and dynamic frameworks and intuitively expresses their similarities and differences. The multi-page search scenario concerns a single query and a single set of documents, making it a simple problem formulation. A multi-page static IR system is illustrated in Figure 2.1. Here, a retrieval system is generating two pages of search results for the query jaguar. This ambiguous query gives results for webpages belonging to the subtopics car, animal and guitar. We suppose that these documents are ranked in decreasing order of their probability of relevance according to the PRP. In this static system, the results on page 2 are unaffected by any interaction that occurs on page 1; a different user searching for the same query would encounter the same results.

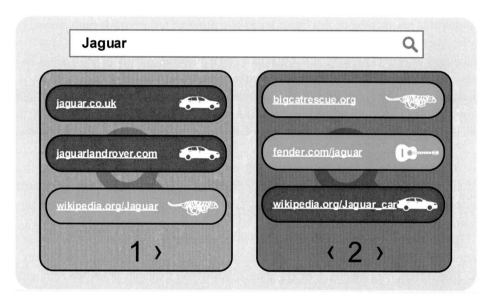

Figure 2.1: Two pages of static search results for the query jaguar, categorized by subtopic.

There are many different ways to perform ranking and retrieval in this environment. A simple, traditional method is the vector space model [210], which treats queries and documents as vectors and ranks documents in decreasing order of their distance from the query. In this scenario there is only one time step whereas dynamic systems operate over many time steps. The scenario could be extended by allowing users to search for multiple queries consecutively in a session. Still, traditional ranking and retrieval models would return the same results regardless of the order of the queries or the behavior of the user and the search engine.

The search scenario given in the example above could be improved by taking into account the relevance feedback from the earlier page and dynamically personalize the results on the latter page. In the next section, we formally examine the weakness of the traditional static information retrieval and reformulate the dynamic information retrieval framework in order to address it.

2.2   STATIC INFORMATION RETRIEVAL

Many traditional problems in IR can be described as static, for instance, adhoc ranking and re-trieval. The solution usually involves using models to find query to document relevance, such as the vector space or BM25 models, topic models such as latent Dirichlet allocation [252], link analysis using methods like PageRank [182] or learning to rank to directly classify an optimal ranking [35]. The paradigm is static in that all the document or feature relevance scores for query terms are generated in advance of retrieval. During retrieval itself, these scores are efficiently found in an inverted index and combined so that a relevant ranking of documents can be made [30]. The scores and thus the rankings are independent of the user's preceding or future actions, queries or the state of the system. Re-calculating the weights based on some real-time user input can be a slow and expensive operation which may involve re-indexing the full or partial corpus. As such, these methods are not able to interactively adjust their scores in a live search setting.

Static IR encompasses problems in information retrieval that are resolved in a single time step or interaction, or multiple independent interactions (represented in Figure 2.2), not requir-ing consideration for how the state of the system has changed following the interaction. Many traditional areas in IR can be described as static, for instance, adhoc ranking and retrieval where document relevance scores for query terms are typically generated in advance of retrieval and fixed. These scores and the rankings they give rise to are independent of the user's preceding or future actions or the state of the system. Re-calculating the scores based on some real-time user input would be a slow and expensive operation.

Figure 2.2: The independent states of static IR.

The objective of a static system is to choose an **action** (or sequence of actions), each of which has an associated **probability of relevance**. The action represents a choice that can be made by the system. For example, the action may be a query suggestion to display to a user or the ranking order of a set of documents for retrieval. Static IR encompasses problems in information retrieval that are resolved in a single time step or interaction, thus we do not need to consider how the state of the system has changed following the interaction. Static IR is not adaptive and so does not satisfy all three of the attributes that define a dynamic IR system. A static system's goal is usually to optimize an objective function or IR metric but only over a single state.

2.2.1   THE RANKING PROBLEM

A well-established static framework for ranking documents is the **Probability Ranking Principle (PRP)**. In 1979, Robertson [198] stated that the effectiveness of a retrieval system is maximized when displaying documents in decreasing order of their estimated probability of relevance $P(R|d,i)$: it is most beneficial to display the document that has the highest probability of relevance first, followed by the second highest and so forth. Here, R is the binary random variable for relevance where $R = 1$ indicates that document d at rank position i is relevant, otherwise $R = 0$. This intuitive result formalized the optimal strategy for displaying ranked documents to users and underlies many static IR models. Nonetheless, this principle also makes the assumption that one is able to accurately estimate the probability of relevance and also that document relevancies are independent of one another, which is not always the case.

The principle is derived from a utility function for the potential loss when retrieving a document, defined as

$$\text{Loss(retrieved|non-relevant)} = \alpha_1 \tag{2.1}$$
$$\text{Loss(not retrieved|relevant)} = \alpha_2 \tag{2.2}$$

for parameters α_1 and α_2. Thus, the expected loss if a document d at rank position i with relevance R has been retrieved is

$$\left(1 - P(R|d,i)\right) \times \alpha_1 \tag{2.3}$$

and if the document was not retrieved, then the expected loss is

$$P(R|d,i) \times \alpha_2. \tag{2.4}$$

Thus, the decision of whether to retrieve document d at rank i is determined by whether

$$P(R|d,i)\alpha_2 > \left(1 - P(R|d,i)\right) \times \alpha_1 \tag{2.5}$$
$$\implies P(R|d,i) > \frac{\alpha_1}{\alpha_2 + \alpha_1}. \tag{2.6}$$

As a result, documents whose probability of relevance $P(R|d,i)$ falls above this threshold utility value should be ranked in decreasing order of said probability, otherwise they should not be ranked as the expected loss becomes positive.

2.2.2   THE DIVERSIFICATION PROBLEM

A drawback of the use of the PRP is that in instances where result diversity is important, it can be shown that ranking according to the PRP is no longer optimal [250]. We illustrate this with an example query `apple`, an ambiguous term that can describe three subtopic search intents `apple computer`, `apple logo` and `apple fruit`. This is captured probabilistically by supposing that there are two classes of users, $user_1$ and $user_2$, where $user_1$ has twice as many members as $user_2$. Users in the $user_1$ class are satisfied with the `apple logo` and `apple computer` subtopics, but not `apple fruit`, while those in the $user_2$ class are only satisfied with the `apple fruit` subtopic. The space of actions here is the set of subtopics which is denoted $\mathcal{A} = \{a_1 = $ `apple logo`$, a_2 = $ `apple computer`$, a_3 = $ `apple fruit`$\}$ and the goal is to choose the best ranking of subtopics.

By setting $R_{a_k} = 1$ if a_k is relevant, and $r_{a_k} = P(R_{a_k} = 1)$, then $r_{a_1} = \frac{2}{3}, r_{a_2} = \frac{2}{3}$ and $r_{a_3} = \frac{1}{3}$. According to the PRP, the subtopics should be ranked in decreasing order of the probability of relevance, giving the ranking sequence $\vec{\mathbf{a}}_{\text{PRP}} = \langle a_1, a_2, a_3 \rangle$. However, intuitively this is not optimal because users belonging to $user_2$ have to reject two subtopics before reaching their preference [65]. This can be explained mathematically by studying the optimization of the diversity-encouraging metric *Expected Search Length*. One can also derive the same conclusion analogously using the equivalent ERR or k-call at n measures [55]. In this scenario, $E[L]_{\vec{\mathbf{a}}}$ is the summation of all possible search lengths L weighted by their respective probabilities, given as

$$E[L]_{\vec{\mathbf{a}}} = \sum_i \left((i-1)P(R_1 = 0, \ldots, R_{i-1} = 0, R_i = 1) \right) \tag{2.7}$$

where R_i is the relevance of the subtopic at rank position i. When assuming subtopics are independent, i.e., $P(R_1 = 0, \ldots, R_i = 1) = P(R_1 = 0) \ldots P(R_{i-1} = 0)P(R_i = 1)$ the expected search length for ranking $\vec{\mathbf{a}}_{\text{PRP}}$ is

$$E[L]_{\vec{\mathbf{a}}_{\text{PRP}}} = 0 \cdot r_{a_1} + 1 \cdot r_{a_2}(1 - r_{a_1}) + 2 \cdot r_{a_3}(1 - r_{a_2})(1 - r_{a_1}) \tag{2.8}$$
$$= 0 \cdot (2/3) + 1 \cdot (2/3)(1/3) + 2 \cdot (1/3)(1/3)(1/3) = \mathbf{8/27} \tag{2.9}$$

and for a diversified ranking $\vec{\mathbf{a}}_{\text{DIV}} = \langle a_1, a_3, a_2 \rangle$ the expected search length is

$$E[L]_{\vec{\mathbf{a}}_{\text{DIV}}} = 0 \cdot (2/3) + 1 \cdot (1/3)(1/3) + 2 \cdot (2/3)(2/3)(1/3) = \mathbf{11/27}. \tag{2.10}$$

Thus, in this case the PRP ranked documents have a shorter expected search path than the diversified ranking. Here, the PRP does lead to the optimal ranking under the independence assumption, but when it is removed this is no longer the case. To see this, expected search length for $\vec{\mathbf{a}}_{\text{PRP}}$ and $\vec{\mathbf{a}}_{\text{DIV}}$ is recalculated but this time without the independence assumption:

$$E[L]_{\vec{\mathbf{a}}_{\text{PRP}}} = 0 \cdot r_{a_1} + 1 \cdot P(R_{a_2} = 1, R_{a_1} = 0) + 2 \cdot P(R_{a_3} = 1, R_{a_2} = 0, R_{a_1} = 0) \tag{2.11}$$
$$= 0 \cdot (2/3) + 1 \cdot 0 + 2 \cdot (1/3) = \mathbf{2/3} \tag{2.12}$$
$$E[L]_{\vec{\mathbf{a}}_{\text{DIV}}} = 0 \cdot (2/3) + 1 \cdot (1/3) + 2 \cdot 0 = \mathbf{1/3}. \tag{2.13}$$

Now it is found that the diversified ranking $\vec{\mathbf{a}}_{\text{DIV}}$ has the shorter expected search length and is thus the optimal ranking, despite the lower probability of relevance for a_3. We next explain how to make use of the relevance feedback to understand how much diversity we need in order to devise an optimal ranking.

2.3   INTERACTIVE INFORMATION RETRIEVAL

An **interactive IR** system is one that extends a static system by incorporating user feedback in the same state. An Interactive IR framework incorporates user feedback. Feedback is an **observation** signal (or a sequence of observations) that is measurable by the search system. These signals can be assigned to three categories:

- In **explicit** relevance feedback, the user is directly solicited for information regarding the relevance of information items, or else their information need preferences. This is usually manifested through an interactive UI that lets users input a binary label or numerical score for items representing their relevance, usefulness or perhaps irrelevance. Alternative methods of collecting feedback include asking users to answer questions regarding their interests for adaptive filtering [84] or allowing users to select item attributes for filtering in faceted e-commerce search [275].

  What these methods have in common is that the user is interrupted during the search process so that the search system may receive feedback. Despite the proven benefits of incorporating explicit relevance labels into the search process found by Salton [211] and Rocchio [201], a wealth of literature has demonstrated the detrimental effect to users that occurs during the collection of the labels. One study found that inexperienced search users preferred a system using implicit relevance feedback over an explicit one, as it reduced the burden of providing feedback [256]. Another found that in UIs incorporating relevance feedback and re-ranking strategies, users favored those that gave them the greatest amount of control, disliking systems that automatically re-ranked results or acted unpredictably [255]. An analysis of search log data found that typically less than 10% of users made use of an available relevance feedback option during searches, even when results were often over 60% better as a result [234]. This reluctance of the user in the submitting of direct input into relevance feedback systems has motivated the development of collecting implicit signals instead.

- In **implicit** relevance feedback, signals observed from natural user interactions with the search system are unobtrusively recorded and interpreted as signals of relevance [138]. Research has found a correlation between relevance and a range of user behaviors, including document reading time [178], webpage dwell time in search [140] and scrolling behavior [90]. A study by Fox et al. found that the right combination of implicit measures could work as effectively as explicit feedback, although many of the signals in their study (such as the session-based features) were less effective [86]. They also found that document clickthroughs proved one of the strongest implicit signals for relevance feedback.

- **Pseudo** relevance feedback systems simulate explicit relevance feedback by assuming that the top k ranked documents in a search ranking are relevant. They then perform conventional relevance feedback to improve search results [39, 258]. Pseudo-relevance feedback has been an active area of research in the last twenty years, usually resulting in improved search performance for single adhoc queries [34, 70].

Once feedback from a user has been observed, an interactive search system can then improve the search experience. Early research in relevance feedback concerned systems that were personalized to each user and dealt with the difficulty for a user to come up with an appropriate query for a given information need. In these systems, after an initial search, a user could explicitly select documents relevant to their information need, resulting in an automatic reformulation of their query into a more relevant one [204]. Recommender systems on e-commerce websites can also be interactive, where explicit and implicit user preferences and ratings allow the user to filter out undesired products and cause the system to adapt to their needs [171, 275]. Modern static search systems also employ interactivity. For instance, query auto-completion [22] systems suggest new queries based on partially typed queries and can also take into account context and past interactions [223]. Query suggestion can also be considered interactive, whereby the search system actively attempts to direct the search session the user is engaged in based on their current query [20].

For clarification, the area of research traditionally known as Interactive Information Retrieval (IIR) has an alternative definition to the interactive IR *conceptual model* discussed in this chapter, despite the similarity in name. IIR research explores the complex sequence of interactions a user may have with a search ranking within the static framework [203], largely motivated by the contradictory results found from conventional Cranfield style evaluation [63] and observational user studies [105]. For the remainder of this lecture any reference to interactive IR instead reflects the interactive framework defined in this chapter.

2.3.1   THE ROCCHIO ALGORITHM

With these features in mind, we extend the vector space example to the interactive scenario in Figure 2.1 by introducing the Rocchio relevance feedback algorithm [201] for interactively re-ranking documents. Here, clicked documents are used as implicit signals of relevance to modify the user's original query. In this case, the system is sensing its environment through the user clicks and responding by changing its ranking. In the first state of this two-state approach, the user enters a query and reviews the set of search results returned by the system, clicking on documents they found relevant. By representing the query and documents using the vector space model, the search system can use the Rocchio formula to modify the query vector so that it moves closer to the relevant documents and further away from the non-relevant documents. The Rocchio formula is given by:

$$q^* = \alpha q + \frac{\beta}{|\mathcal{D}_r|} \sum_{d \in \mathcal{D}_r} d - \frac{\gamma}{|\mathcal{D}_{nr}|} \sum_{d \in \mathcal{D}_{nr}} d \qquad (2.14)$$

where q and q^* are respectively the original query vector and its modified version under Rocchio. $\mathcal{D}_r$ and $\mathcal{D}_{nr}$ are the set of relevant and non-relevant documents (as determined by the user

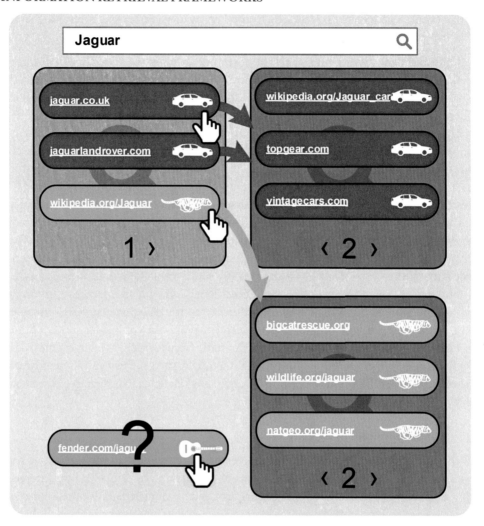

Figure 2.3: Clicked webpages lead to the personalization of the second page of results based on the subtopic clicked on page 1 of the ranking in Figure 2.1, but subtopic guitar is no longer represented.

clicks) and d is the document vector. α, β and γ weight the effect of the original query, relevant documents and non-relevant documents on query modification. In the second state, ranking and retrieval occurs using the modified query which usually leads to improved recall.

When we apply the Rocchio algorithm to our static ranking example in Figure 2.1(a), we can personalize the second page of search results based on the user's subtopic preference. For instance, if a user flagged car related webpages as relevant on page 1 (or the system observed clicks on those webpages), then the second page of results can be updated as shown in Figure 2.3(a).

Likewise, if their preference is the subtopic `animal` then the algorithm will respond appropriately to give the ranking in Figure 2.3(b). This is a user targeted improvement over the static ranker's second page in Figure 2.1(b) which continued to display a mix of subtopics.

A problem with this interactive approach is that it does not account for users who are not interested in the two subtopics found on page 1 (there is one webpage categorized in the `guitar` subtopic on page 2 in Figure 2.1(b)). A user interested in guitars using this search system may not discover the `guitar` related webpage on page 2 due to the system re-ranking those results following feedback on page 1, degrading the search experience. In the next chapter we complete our discussion of the conceptual model by introducing dynamic IR in full and investigate how it can help us resolve the situation in this example.

2.3.2 INTERACTIVE PROBABILITY RANKING PRINCIPLE

The static PRP framework has been extended to an interactive version known as the **Probability Ranking Principle in Interactive IR (IIR-PRP)** [87]. Here, the assumption of document independence is removed by the definition of a utility function that explicitly incorporates dependence. This utility models a user that makes *choices* while browsing a ranked list of search results. For each choice the benefit and cost to the user is quantified, as well as the probability of the user accepting the choice and also the probability that the choice is relevant. For instance, in adhoc ranking the cost may be the effort required to read a document snippet and the benefit would be the knowledge gained.

This utility can be described as the expected benefit of document d_i (document d ranked at position i) given as

$$\mathrm{E}[d_i] = \omega(i) + P(R_i|d,i)\big(b_i\alpha_i + (1-b_i)\beta_i\big) \tag{2.15}$$

where $\omega(i)$ is the effort required to reach rank i, α_i is the utility gain when the document is relevant and β_i is the utility loss when the document is not relevant. The bias value b_i is the probability that the document at rank i is the correct choice, i.e., that $R_i = 1$. When determining the expected benefit of a ranked list of M documents, the overall utility is

$$\mathrm{E}[\langle d_1,\ldots,d_M\rangle] = \sum_{i=1}^{M}\left(\prod_{j=1}^{i-1}\big(1 - P(R_i|d,j)\big)\right)\big(\omega(i) + P(R_i|d,i)(b_i\alpha_i + (1-b_i)\beta_i)\big). \tag{2.16}$$

Fuhr [87] shows that when optimizing over Eq. (2.16), the optimal ranking policy is to rank documents in decreasing order of the utility score

$$\varrho(d_i) = \big(b_i\alpha_i + (1-b_i)\beta_i\big) + \frac{\omega(i)}{P(R_i|d,i)}. \tag{2.17}$$

In summary, the Rocchio algorithm [201] uses explicit feedback to improve the user's query. Recommender systems, ad selection and query auto completion are examples of modern systems that incorporate feedback to improve performance. Also pertinent to research in both interactive IR and dynamic IR is the use of alternative user interfaces. Over the years many such interfaces have been researched, such as grouping techniques [273], 3D visualization [102] and real-time responsiveness [87, 192], often with mixed user success. Attempting to engage the user in directly interacting with the search interface (such as with drop down menus [29]) or altering their expectations (by changing the ranking [219]) can prove detrimental. In early relevance feedback research, it was found that interactively manipulating the search results was less satisfactory to users than offering them alternative query suggestions [143] and likewise with automatic query expansion [202]. Users appeared to be less happy with systems that automatically adjusted rankings for them and more satisfied when given control over how and when the system performed relevance feedback [255].

2.4   DYNAMIC INFORMATION RETRIEVAL

A Dynamic IR system responds to the dynamics of its real world setting so that it can achieve its goal. Such systems are resistant to adverse change or error and are able to learn and adapt.

Dynamic IR is a progression from static IR and interactive IR in that it deals with the complexity of user interaction by operating over multiple states and making use of user feedback. The states may represent multiple queries in a search session, multiple sessions in a user's search history, different users in a search log and so on. Each state may make use of a static method to generate a search ranking, but the key difference in an interactive system (rather than repeated use of a static system) is that it can adapt to the user after each state, perhaps by re-ranking results [238], omitting duplicates or offering query suggestions, improving and personalizing the search experience throughout.

A **state** represents an interaction with the search system that is distinct from other interactions but belongs to the same search task, for example a sequence of impressions in session search. It is possible that a search system may remain in the same *state* across multiple states, for example, a user refreshing their browser. Generally, an IR system will operate over $1 \leq t \leq T$ states with T being potentially infinite. The states may represent multiple queries in a search session, multiple sessions in a user's search history, different users in a search log and so on. Multiple states may also occur within an individual webpage where there is dynamically changing content. An interactive system may begin by using a static method but will then continue to adapt to the user after each state, with new web capable devices and IR interfaces leading to the availability of different user interactions and feedback signals.

2.4.1   REINFORCEMENT LEARNING VS. DYNAMIC IR MODELING

During information seeking, users explore the information space by inputting queries, examining retrieved documents and clicking on documents that they are interested in. The retrieval system works in concert to try to find relevant documents that satisfy the user. A central argument of this

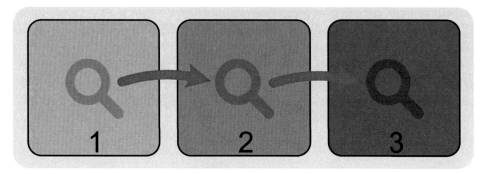

Figure 2.4: Dependent states in dynamic IR.

lecture is that an effective system should adjust its search strategy according to user feedback on the previously retrieved results.

Intuitively, such a problem should be solved in a trial-and-error **Reinforcement Learning (RL)** setting. Reinforcement learning algorithms are designed to maximize some cumulative reward by making actions in their environment and learning the outcome through a feedback signal. Unlike supervised learning which is trained over a labeled dataset, RL algorithms can only observe the correctness of their action after it has been made, and it is often the case that observations cannot be made on those actions not chosen at each time step. Reinforcement Learning models are stochastic models assuming the Markov property, where the system's current state is based on the previous states in a non-deterministic manner [179]. They fit well in session search, where a search engine agent selects its actions (the document rankings) based on its past experiences and current status.

RL algorithms match well with the trial-and-error setting present in Dynamic IR systems: the algorithm learns from repeated, explorative actions until it is optimized for maximizing some reward. The learner (which is a dynamic agent) learns from its dynamic interactions with the world, rather than from a labeled dataset as is the case in supervised learning. In such a setting, a stochastic model assumes that the system's current state depends on the previous state and action in a non-deterministic manner [179].

Among the various models in the RL family, the partially observable Markov decision process [231] has been applied recently to IR problems, including session search [169], document re-ranking [120, 277] and advertisement bidding [269]. In this chapter, the background to this model is explored and then applied to session search.

2.4.2   MARKOV DECISION PROCESS

A system that changes, whether it be over a period of time or over a sequence of states, could be defined as a stochastic process [241]. The process can be simplified by making it memoryless whereby the current state is dependent only on its previous state [173]. This is known as the **Markov Property** and is used to define a **Markov Chain (MC)** [179], a model for systems whose state depends only upon its previous state (as represented in Figure 2.5). A Markov chain can be defined as a tuple $(\mathcal{S}, \mathcal{T})$, where $\mathcal{S}$ is a set of states and $\mathcal{T}$ is the state transition function. $\mathcal{T}(s, s')$ denotes the probability of transition from state s to state s'. The Markov chain is a dynamic process that starts from an initial probability distribution over the random variable for the state S, then iterates according to $P(S = s') = P(S = s)\mathcal{T}(s, s')$. Typically, an MC will converge to an equilibrium distribution when $\mathcal{T}$ satisfies certain conditions.

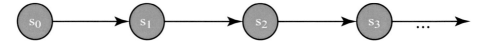

Figure 2.5: States in a Markov chain.

A **Markov Decision Process (MDP)** is a stochastic decision process with the Markov property. An agent takes inputs from the environment and outputs actions; the actions in turn influence the other states of the environment according to the transition probability distribution. MDPs assign immediate rewards for taking an action at a state. Formally, an MDP is a tuple [27] $(\mathcal{S}, \mathcal{A}, \mathcal{R}, \mathcal{T}, \gamma)$, made up of:

States The state $s \in \mathcal{S}$ describes the status or environment that the agent is in at a given moment in time.

Actions The action $a \in \mathcal{A}$ describes the possible changes that the agent can make at a given moment of time given the current state.

Reward The reward function $\mathcal{R}(s, a)$ is the reward of taking action a when in state s.

State Transition Function The transition probability $\mathcal{T}(s, a, s')$ denotes the probability of transition from state s to state s' triggered by an action a.

Discount The discount parameter $\gamma \in [0, 1]$ can be set as a discount factor for future rewards.

The goal of an MDP is to find an optimal policy, i.e., the best sequence of actions $a_0, a_1, \dots$ that maximizes $\sum_{i=0}^{\infty} \gamma^i \mathcal{R}(s_i, a_i)$, the long-term accumulated reward which sums up all (discounted) rewards from the beginning to the end of the process. A typical MDP structure is shown in Figure 2.6.

An optimal solution to an MDP can be found using **dynamic programming**, which is the process of breaking down a difficult problem into sub-problems that can be solved independently, then combining their solutions to form the overall solution to the main problem. For an MDP, this means choosing the optimal action to take at a particular time step in order to maximize the immediate reward. The Markov property ensures that rewards are not dependent on previous rewards, and so an optimal policy across many time steps can be found.

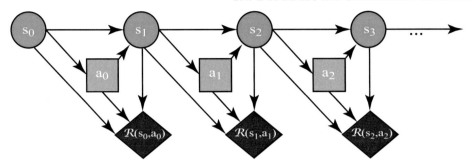

Figure 2.6: The Markov Decision Process influence diagram.

An optimal policy, which is a sequence of mapping from states to actions, maximizes the reward in the dynamic system. There are two well-established dynamic programming algorithms for finding optimal policies in MDPs: *value iteration* is the case where the expected overall state of the dynamic system is set and then optimization occurs backward until an optimal sequence of decisions is made from the starting point; likewise, in *policy iteration* the optimization occurs from the starting point until the model's reward converges [25]. Both value iteration and policy iteration are based on the Bellman equation [24]:

$$V(s) = \max_a \left[\mathcal{R}(s, a) + \gamma \sum_{s'} \mathcal{T}(s, a, s') V(s') \right]. \tag{2.18}$$

In addition, there are also two well-known variants to this solution: Q-Learning [251] which shows how to build an optimal policy function that doesn't require knowledge of the underlying model; and Temporal Difference learning [239], where Monte Carlo sampling is combined with an MDP framework to predict the next state and update the model parameters.

MDPs bring actions into the family of stochastic Markov models. Hence it is able to model interactions between the user and the search engine. Its reward function also provides a goal for the search engine to make decisions in the long term and can lead the entire information seeking process to eventually meet the user's information need. MDPs are used in situations where the states are completely observable. In the case where states are hidden, for instance if the user's information need is modeled as the state, then the MDP might be inadequate for this purpose.

2.4.3 PARTIALLY OBSERVABLE MARKOV DECISION PROCESS

A **Partially Observable Markov Decision Process (POMDP)** is a variant MDP that takes into account that the agent may not know which state it is currently in. Generally speaking, it models an agent's belief about its current state based on observations of its environment and the actions available to it. After taking an action and receiving a reward, the agent makes a new observation and updates its belief about its state. The POMDP formulation allows the agent to optimize which

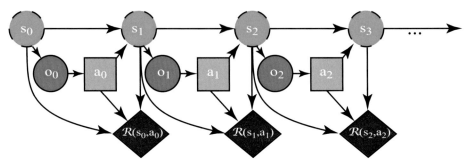

Figure 2.7: The POMDP influence diagram, where states are no longer observable but their observations are.

action to take depending on its belief state. The POMDP theoretical model can be represented by the tuple $(\mathcal{S}, \mathcal{A}, \mathcal{R}, \mathcal{T}, \gamma, \Omega, \Theta, r, b)$. The states, actions, rewards, transition state function and discount are defined as for an MDP, the new elements are:

Observations In the POMDP framework, agents cannot determine which state they are currently in directly, but they can make an observation $o \in \Omega$ which gives some indication of the state they are in.

Observation Function The observation function $\Theta(s, a, o) = P(o|s, a)$ determines the probability of making a particular observation given the hidden state of the agent and the action taken.

Belief The belief is the probability that the agent is in a given state and is given by the function $r(s) = P(S = s)$.

Belief Update Function The agent maintains a belief about its hidden state given by r. After making an action and receiving an observation, the belief can be updated using the belief update function $r'(s) = b(r(s), a, o)$ which can be estimated by $\sum_{o \in \Omega} P(r'(s)|r(s), a, o) P(o|a, r(s))$.

In a POMDP, because the agent does not know which state it is in, the reward is estimated by marginalizing over the belief state. As such, the goal of a POMDP is to find an optimal policy of actions that maximizes the overall expected reward $\sum_{i=0}^{\infty} \gamma^i \sum_{s \in \mathcal{S}} r(s) \mathcal{R}(s_i, a_i)$. A typical POMDP structure is shown in Figure 2.7.

In a POMDP the state is unknown, and observations of the state may be misleading or not convey enough information. The solution to a POMDP is made by mapping it onto a continuous state Markov decision process, where the continuous state is the belief state. Through such a transformation, the value function of a POMDP can be expressed in a recursive form similar to the Bellman equation used for an MDP in Eq. (2.18):

$$V\left(r(s)\right) = \max_a \left[\mathcal{R}\left(r(s), a\right) + \omega \sum_{o \in \Omega} P\left(o'|a, r(s)\right) V\left(r'\right) \right]. \tag{2.19}$$

Here, potential observations of the state are marginalized over and r' is the belief state in the next iteration given by the belief update function $b\left(r(s), a, o\right)$. The belief update is the most important aspect of the POMDP as it allows one to estimate the state transitions occurring while not being able to directly observe them.

When determining an optimal policy for a POMDP, we can use dynamic programming techniques to find the optimal decision for each time step. In dynamic programming, we use a value function that allows us to use value or policy iteration algorithms and calculate the utility of the decision at each moment in time. By iterating backward (or forward depending on the algorithm), we can optimize over all possible outcomes and determine the best policy. Algorithms have been proposed to solve such problems [123], although many meet with issues such as intractability and the curse of dimensionality, especially for practical problems and particularly when applied to the kinds of problems seen in IR which can involve millions of states, actions and observations.

2.4.4 BANDITS MODELS

Multi-armed bandits [32, 89] is a prominent paradigm to study the tradeoff between acquisition and usage of information, a.k.a., explore-exploit tradeoff. It has been applied to study problems on how to interpret clicks when several search results or news articles are presented at once (e.g., [127, 270]), how to ensure diversity in search results [190], how to use known information about similarity between the actions and/or users (e.g., *tree bandits* [183, 225], *Lipschitz bandits* [33, 142] and *Gaussian Process bandits* [236]), how to incorporate budget constraints of advertisers [19, 245], and many others.

Here an algorithm repeatedly chooses actions (*arms*) from a fixed set of arms, and observes the reward for the chosen arm only. The name comes from a fictional scenario where a gambler faces several slot machines ("one-armed bandits") which look the same but may differ in payoffs. On a high level, there are three main versions, depending on how the rewards are generated: each arm follows a Markov chain with a known transition matrix and observable states [89]; rewards for each arm are i.i.d. samples from a fixed distribution [12]; and all rewards are chosen by an adversary [14]. Two important algorithmic techniques with i.i.d. samples are Upper Confidence Bounds (UCB) [12] and Thompson Sampling [243]. Both techniques have been thoroughly studied, lead to much follow-up work and are well-suited to various extensions (see the survey [32] for background and references).

The main applications of them are in the domains of web search, ad placement and news recommendations. Here "actions" available to an algorithm correspond to which search results, ads, or news articles to display to a given user, and/or to different ways these items may be presented (e.g., in terms of font or placement on the page). A typical "reward" depends on whether the chosen item(s) have been clicked on. Reward can also incorporate other observable signals, such as "conversion" (whether a user bought something) or "dwell time" (time spent by the user). Each user usually comes with a "context": a feature vector which describes known demographics, geography or history of past interactions with the system, so contextual bandits approaches may be used.

2.5 MODELING DYNAMIC IR

Recent advances in the field of dynamic IR have led to the formulation of a framework for dynamic IR [228]. Like with the previous frameworks, a core component is the definition of a utility function that describes the costs and benefits of choosing actions. The interactive IR framework was previously defined as exhibiting dependency features, but was only capable of locally optimizing for a single state at a time. In contrast, the optimization of a dynamic system must find the optimal sequence of actions for all future interactions. A result of this is that the utility of an individual state may be reduced so that gains can be made in the utility at a future state.

A dynamic framework has access to the feedback signal obtained in the previous interaction. This is achieved by marginalizing the dynamic utility function over the space of all possible observations. When doing this the **observation likelihood function** $P(o|a, r)$ must be specified.

Thus, the **utility function for dynamic information retrieval** can be defined as

$$U_D(r_t, t) = \max_{a_t \in \mathcal{A}} \left[U_S(a_t, r_t) + \omega(t) \sum_{o \in \mathcal{O}} P(o|a_t, r_t) U_D(\tau(a_t, r_t, o), t+1) \right] \qquad (2.20)$$

where $U_D(r_T, T) = \max_{a_T \in \mathcal{A}} \left[U_S(a_T, r_T) \right]$ is the static optimization of the final state, and each of the components is described in Table 2.1. Thus, the objective is to find, through backward induction, the optimal sequence of actions that maximizes the **dynamic utility** U_D given in Eq. (2.20).

The eight elements of the Dynamic IR framework: $a, r, U_S, t, o, \tau, P(o|a, r)$ and $\omega(t)$, also shown in Table 2.1, are also the elements that define a POMDP, and the dynamic utility function is its corresponding Bellman equation. Intuitively this makes sense, like a POMDP the dynamic IR framework finds an optimal Markovian sequence of actions to maximize a reward (here the static utility) subject to discounting (with ω). The state of the system (the underlying document relevance) is unknown but a belief state (the probability of relevance) is updated according to observations. The key difference from a POMDP is that for dynamic IR there is no defined transition probability between states due to the assumption that the hidden relevance of each document does not change throughout the search task.

Here, each of the components in the dynamic IR framework are analyzed to give additional insight:

Relevance   As with any framework in information retrieval, the overall aim is to retrieve relevant information items and present them to the user. The intrinsic "relevance" of an information item is

Table 2.1: Elements of the *Dynamic IR* framework

Element	Description	Examples
a	Action	Query suggestion, ranking of documents
r	Relevance	Query or document relevance
t	State	Impression, rank position, page
o	Observation (feedback) signal	Click, e-commerce transaction
τ	Probability of Relevance Update Function	Rocchio, multi-variate Gaussian
$P(o|a,r)$	Probability of Observation Function	Click model, eye-tracking distribution
U_S	Individual State Static Utility	DCG, ERR
ω	Path-Discount Function	Geometric, path-based

an unknown quality and the subject of most of the research in IR. In the Dynamic IR framework any document relevance scoring method can be used.

The relevance update function τ is more difficult to define as it depends specifically on the action and observation space of the Dynamic IR task. This dependence allows τ to adapt to the hidden relevance preferences of the user over the course of the search process. It may not always be clear how to update the relevance score based on a given observation, the most straightforward setting for τ can simply be to set $r_a = 0$ for actions already chosen by the IR system. Because τ enforces the temporal dependency, it is the most important aspect in the dynamic utility because without it the utility is static.

States   Typically, the states in a Dynamic IR task represent distinct interactions occurring in a linear time order. In these cases $\omega(t)$ may take a value between 0 and 1 or be set to a monotonically decreasing function that favorably weights the utility scores of immediate states. Setting $\omega(1) = 1$ and $\omega(t) = 0$ for $t > 1$ gives the static and interactive scenarios.

Alternatively, a non-linear sequence of interactions (or *search path*) can be modeled as Yang and Lad did with their session-based utility function [265]. For instance in session search, a search path represents a particular sequence of documents examined by the user and the query reformulations made. For the Dynamic IR framework, the state t may instead represent a specific search path, and so $\omega(t)$ could be interpreted as the likelihood of this path rather than an explicit discount, penalizing improbable search paths and rewarding likely ones.

The time horizon T dictates the number of advance states to optimize for. A large time horizon will lead to explorative action strategies that benefit later states. In the examples in this chapter, T is set to 2.

Actions   The action space is what distinguishes search tasks from one another and it is the size of this space that dictates the complexity of optimizing over the dynamic utility function. For example, the action space in query suggestion or document ranking is potentially infinite whereas

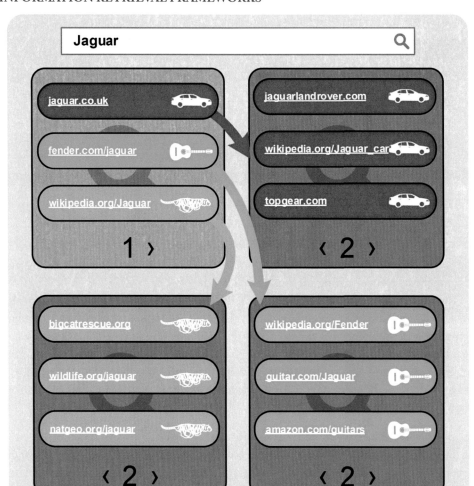

Figure 2.8: The first page ranking has been diversified so that the search system is better able to learn the user's second page preference, improving the overall search experience for all users.

the space of available advertisements in an ad selection problem may be small and finite. Along with τ, the setting of the static utility U_S is important for determining the desirable features of the optimal actions, such as results diversification.

Observations   The observation space is dependent on the action space, its elements representing the user's response to system actions. Each observation must contain some signal of relevance or search intent, otherwise $\tau(a, r, o) = \tau(a, r)$ and there would be no temporal dependency. In some cases the value of the observation likelihood is simply $P(o|a, r) = r$, for instance in search tasks where accurate explicit relevance feedback is guaranteed. Otherwise, in most situations the observations will be click-related and thus the observation probability is the probability of click.

Dynamic Utility   Through the recursive evaluation of the utility function, we cannot only learn the optimal sequence of actions to make in the dynamic system, but also learn the optimal action for each possible observation at each state. If one were to store these in a lookup table ahead of deployment, then the dynamic system would be immediately responsive to user feedback and able to cater to a population of users.

Dynamic IR is a natural evolution of the described static and interactive models. As is the case with an interactive system, a dynamic system may collect feedback from a static system and respond accordingly. A key difference is how the objective of the system is optimized and defined; in interactive retrieval only immediate rewards for the current states are considered, whereas in dynamic retrieval the overall reward is prioritized. As a result, the action chosen at each time step in a dynamic system is made in consideration of all past and future interactions. The anticipation of future interactions and rewards in pursuit of the overall goal may affect the behavior of the system during its early states and we cover this more fully under Exploration and Exploitation in Chapter 3.

In summary, the differences between the three types of IR system in this conceptual model are: static systems are those that operate over a single state or otherwise multiple states which are independent of one another. Interactive systems extend static systems by introducing local dependency from one state to the next and optimizing for individual goals per state. A dynamic system extends an interactive system by focusing on a single goal that forces dependency across all states. In this book, Dynamic IR is defined as the modeling of adaptive, responsive, goal-oriented information retrieval systems.

CHAPTER 3

Dynamic IR for a Single Query

Online learning to rank is defined as *"a continuous cycle of interactions between users and a search engine, in which the search engine's goal is to provide the best possible search results at all times"* [107]. The field was first motivated as an extension of the **learning to rank** framework, the application of supervised machine learning algorithms to the space of search tasks. As with other areas of IR, the goal in learning to rank is to find an optimal ranking of documents for an information need. In this case, document relevance labels (generated by assessors or otherwise) are used to train a classifier (such as an SVM) to identify relevant documents, or optimal rankings of documents, for validation in a test set. A range of document, query, session and user features are typically used to train the classifier [163]. The learning to rank classification of relevance labels or regression of ranking scores fall broadly into three categories:

Pointwise The binary relevance label of individual documents are learned using a classifier [42].

Pairwise Instead of learning a direct relevance label, the correct order of pairs of documents is learned, as is the case with the well-known RankSVM algorithm [121].

Listwise IR measures such as nDCG or MAP are directly optimized over lists of documents, as in the widely used LambdaMART algorithm [35].

A barrier to effective learning to rank is the acquisition of relevance labels, many of which are needed to train accurate, reliable and generalizable ranking systems. A common solution is to use explicit labels provided by users or else noisy, implicit labels such as clicks found in abundance in search logs. In whatever form relevance labels are obtained, they come at some cost and also vary in their informativeness. Active and semi-supervised learning techniques can therefore be employed to minimize such costs and maximize the learning potential of training sets, perhaps dynamically, over time. Once trained, a ranking classifier can be difficult to maintain, particularly in light of shifting search intents and new documents. Online learning to rank has been developed as a solution to these problems.

In online learning to rank, feedback signals from the user are used as relevance labels and used to update the ranking algorithm when received. The search ranking may change over time in response to this feedback, gradually converging on an optimal ranking that is informed by user input. Such systems can generate results targeted to users that can adapt over time and minimize the overheads of expensive label collecting. Examples of online learning to rank applications include ranking and retrieval [108], document diversification [189], evaluation [188], news article recommendation [157] and ad display [58].

It is clear that online learning to rank is the application of dynamic IR to the search ranking problem. In this case, the query and information need are fixed, but the user at each time step is dynamic (in that online learning to rank occurs over a population of users). The overall objective is to learn the relevance of a set of documents or learn a ranking that optimizes a given evaluation metric. The feedback signals are the user clicks, ratings, comparisons or any other sign of relevance obtained after each search.

In this chapter, we cover each of the areas described in more detail before finally surveying the literature on online learning to rank. We start by discussing a related precursor to the field, information filtering the case of online learning to rank for a single user. This allows us to cover relevant subtopics such as relevance feedback and active learning, both of which are important to information filtering, online learning to rank and dynamic IR, in more detail. This leads into an overview of reinforcement learning with a focus on the multi-armed bandit theory and finally a survey of the online learning to rank literature with its links to dynamic IR and reinforcement learning.

3.1   INFORMATION FILTERING

Information Filtering (IF) is an IR problem that has been studied for several decades. The scenario concerns a user with a specific information need/s accessing information items over time. At each time step, the user may use the information items or ignore them and they are usually replaced by different items in the next time step. The items may be retrieved from a static corpus or a stream of documents that changes with each time step. IF broadly falls into two categories: **Active**—where documents are sought out from a corpus to display to the user; and **Passive**—where documents are removed from a stream of documents so that only those that are relevant are retained.

Applying a threshold to ranked documents (i.e., selecting the top 5) is an efficient and commonly used matching method in IF. There are many other methods, most of which fall into three areas:

Content Based Features from a user's profile/information need can be matched to those found in documents [172].

Sociological Documents found relevant by users are recommended to other users that share similar features [257]. This type of information filtering led to the development of modern recommender systems which are covered in more detail in Chapter 5.

Rule Based Logical matching rules are used to remove or retain documents. These rules may be defined by the user, the system designer or learned dynamically over time through thresholding [200].

Early applications of IF included search result filters, email spam detectors, product and academic article recommendation. Modern examples include news and RSS feeds, microblog and social media streams.

Belkin and Croft described IF as *"the process of determining which profiles have a high probability of being satisfied by particular object from the incoming stream,"* noting that the difference between IF and traditional IR was the dynamic document set where documents are retrieved (or removed in filtering) for a stable (static) user profile [23]. The corpus is dynamic, whether it be a stream of documents or even a static corpus where previously retrieved documents are ignored in future time steps. The user profile is the internal "state" of the system, which can be sensed and updated over time but nonetheless is present at each iteration. This profile is simply another representation of an information need or an extended form of query. The feedback in an IF system is thus used to update the user profile, which can be achieved in a number of ways. For instance, a form containing a series of questions can determine appropriate user features [84] or the documents deemed relevant by a user (through explicit feedback) can be combined into a pseudo-document that is matched to new documents to determine their relevance [28].

IF featured as a topic of research at the TREC conference for several years in the adaptive filtering track [197]. Here, adaptive filtering was differentiated from "batch" filtering by the limitation that user profiles had to be constructed from relevance feedback over time, rather than already predefined for filtering over, thus adapting to the user. For instance, it had already been shown that the sequential feedback of document relevance over time led to information filtering systems that performed as effectively as a system that received all of the feedback at once, and could also account for topic drift [8]. As a result, the track encouraged the submission of dynamic models for IF and the application of machine learning techniques. For instance, the use of a perceptron for the online learning of document relevance over time [49], and Robertson's work on dynamically altering thresholds for filtering documents that allowed active exploration of new documents through relevance feedback [200]. Nonetheless, it was only in later years that the performance of the algorithms in the adaptive filtering track proved beneficial in a practical setting and the track has not been repeated since 2002.

Recent advances in IF have focused on introducing concepts such as risk and diversity into retrieval. For instance, Zhang et al. investigated using cosine similarity to optimize filtering for improving novelty and decreasing redundancy in an adaptive filtering system [279]. Related to this was Zhang's later work on combining IF techniques (such as the Rocchio algorithm and linear regression) according to their bias and variance at different stages of the IF task [278]. Their dynamic method learned which techniques were optimally applicable at each stage of IF so as to improve the overall performance of the IF system.

3.1.1   RELEVANCE FEEDBACK

In order for an IF system to be adaptive, it must acquire relevance signals from the user so that it can update its internal model of the user's preferences. These signals can be directly collected from the user in the form of relevance feedback [204] which has already been identified as a core component of a dynamic IR system. In Chapter 2 we introduced the three different types of relevance feedback: **explicit**, **implicit** and **pseudo**.

Clicks are the most popular form of implicit feedback used in IR research, the low cost of collecting them means they can be found in abundance in search logs. Numerous studies have demonstrated the correlation that clicks share with document relevance [44], although usually at the cost of poorer search results quality (for instance, lower recall) when tested against explicit relevance feedback [128]. The general finding with these studies is that clicks are informative but biased. The common cause of this bias is attributed to rank position [122], although SERP features such as URL length and caption readability [59], or session level features such as the impression position and the average number of documents examined [117], have also been shown to affect the probability that a user clicks on a document.

When using clicks from search logs to help build and improve search systems, rank bias can be taken into account by modeling the clicks using a number of **click models** [57]. These are probabilistic models that represent a user's typical behavior with an SERP, typically modeling the likelihood that a user will examine a snippet or click on a document. Three simple and well-known models are the *examination hypothesis*, *cascade* [69] and *dependent* click models [97].

In the examination hypothesis model, the probability of a click C given a document d ranked at position i is given by

$$P(C|d,i) = P(R|d) \times b_i \tag{3.1}$$

where R is the hidden relevance of d (typically a binary label of relevant or not relevant) and $b_i \in [0,1]$ is a parameter representing the *bias* of the ranking position.

In the cascade model,

$$P(C|d,i) = P(R|d) \prod_{j=1}^{i-1} \left(1 - P(R|d_j)\right) \tag{3.2}$$

where d_j is the document ranked at position j. Here, the probability of a click depends on the relevance of documents ranked at higher positions, modeling a user who examines documents in a list from top to bottom and leaves the search results page after finding a relevant document. An observation of a click means that all documents ranked above must have been skipped by the user.

In the dependent click model,

$$P(C|d,i) = P(R|d) \prod_{j=1}^{i-1} \left(1 - P(R|d_j) + b_j P(R|d_j)\right) \tag{3.3}$$

which extends the cascade model to include the effect of rank bias on the probability of clicks on higher ranked documents.

Click models are an active area of research, with recently developed models incorporating sequential decision making through Markov chains [96], dynamic Bayesian networks [54] and, related to the work in this thesis, a POMDP to model more complex user interactions [100].

When carefully considered, clicks have been successfully utilized in a range of IR research projects. For instance, Shen et al. combined clicks with a statistical language model to improve retrieval in an interactive system that contextualized search results for users [218]. In a similar fashion, user profiles can be built up over time by using clicks in a user's search history to personalize search results [238]. An effective application of implicit relevance feedback is in image search re-ranking [110], which is a difficult search problem without relevance feedback. Finally, in relation to the work in this chapter, clicks have also been successfully used as relevance signals in online interleaved evaluation [51] and as labels in learning to rank [4].

One of the three characteristics of a dynamic system is the procurement of an interaction signal. As described, this signal can take many forms, with explicit signals being more accurate but affecting the quality of the search experience, and implicit signals needing careful treatment to be effective. As evidenced throughout this lecture, many dynamic IR systems use clicks as their form of feedback and we find that this is usually the case with online learning to rank as well. Many IF systems tend to use explicit forms of feedback due to the nature of the filtering system and the increased quality of the signal, which is vital for personalization for a single user.

3.1.2   ACTIVE LEARNING

Feedback is vital to dynamic IR systems but it can be costly to obtain, either in an economic sense with relevance judgments or through encumbering a user of a search system. Particularly in learning to rank or information filtering, explicit feedback labels can be worth this additional cost. Research in **active learning** seeks to minimize this cost by only acquiring feedback on training labels that can help achieve the greatest accuracy and efficiency in learning an optimal ranking function [217].

In adaptive filtering, stream-based selective sampling is used to determine the optimal documents to display to a user from a stream of documents, balancing the choice of explorative documents that help build the user's profile and exploitative documents that the user will find relevant [280]. Filtering thresholds may also be selected using an active learning approach to collect explicit relevance judgments [200] or by filtering over more documents when a topic change has been detected [152].

In learning to rank (as well as batch information filtering), pool-based active learning techniques are used instead, where labels are sought from an existing collection of unlabeled training instances, seeking out those with the most uncertainty of their true label. For instance, an early listwise learning to rank algorithm used an SVM combined with a selective sampling strategy to learn over the most ambiguous training instances [268]. In recent work, sensitive samples were identified by applying varying amounts of noise to samples and determining which perturbed the ranking decision the most [38], areas with the lowest data density [37] or as an addition to

RankSVM to determine the most informative labels for learning [77]. Active learning has also been used to identify representative query document pairs and features by being paired with a principle components analysis algorithm to increase the efficiency of learning to rank [36].

The combination of adaptive filtering with learning to rank using active learning is effectively the definition of online learning to rank, where the relevance of documents is learned over time via feedback through the careful sequential selection of informative and relevant documents. As covered in more detail later in this chapter, reinforcement learning methods such as multi-armed bandits are typically used for this, yet we observe similarities between the techniques in the active learning literature. For instance, the balance of exploration vs. exploitation [280], the selection of labels with the most uncertainty in a sequential algorithm [64, 155] and the minimization of regret as an operational goal [48].

Active learning's focus on the long-term improvement of a system through intelligent selection and feedback makes it an addition to the dynamic IR tool set. Aside from its application in information filtering and learning to rank, it has been used successfully in general relevance feedback research to minimize the user effort in providing labels for web search [220, 244], in particular for difficult to rank queries [259] and image retrieval [72].

3.1.3   MULTI-PAGE SEARCH

Multi-page search is a special case of information filtering applicable to modern search systems. The scenario concerns the ranking of documents over multiple pages of search results where documents are retrieved for a single query, ranked and then segregated into pages of M documents. On each page, a user may examine and click on documents and the goal is use this feedback to improve the rankings over all pages of search. This scenario is briefly explored in the context of static, interactive and dynamic IR in our example in Chapter 2.

Like with information filtering, a user profile is learned using implicit feedback so that the results for the current query can be improved for the user [139]. The use of implicit feedback reduces the disruption to the user and can be implemented on the server-side or even in the user's browser as a plug-in to preserve privacy [68]. Due to the limited number of pages from which the search system can typically learn from, actively learning over the right balance of speculative and relevant search results is vital, as well as the understanding that over the course of the multi-page interaction, not only is the search system learning from the user, but that the opposite is also true [221].

We complete the example from Chapter 2 by formulating a dynamic solution to the multi-page search problem [120]. We model the relevance of each document as a multivariate Gaussian distribution

$$R \sim \mathcal{N}(\vec{\mathbf{r}}, \Sigma) \tag{3.4}$$

where R is their collective random variable, $\vec{\mathbf{r}}$ the vector of mean relevance scores and Σ the covariance matrix over the documents. $\vec{\mathbf{r}}$ may be set as any relevance score and Σ may be set using document similarity or other correlation scores. If $\vec{r}$ represents a probability of relevance, then the distribution can be set as a *truncated* multivariate Gaussian bounded between 0 and 1. If it is not possible to define the distribution of a relevance score, then the distribution of the mean of multiple relevance scoring techniques can be derived, resulting in an approximately Gaussian distribution that incorporates multiple signals of relevance.

Modeling the relevance distribution in this way allows us to conditionally update the probabilities of relevance $\vec{r}$ based on click observations. For a given rank action $\vec{a}_t$ (which includes both clicked and non-clicked documents in the ranking), the remaining non-ranked documents are denoted as $\backslash\vec{a}_t$ and the distribution parameters are partitioned as

$$\vec{r} = \begin{bmatrix} \vec{r}_{\backslash\vec{a}_t} \\ \vec{r}_{\vec{a}} \end{bmatrix} \qquad \Sigma = \begin{bmatrix} \Sigma_{\backslash\vec{a}_t\backslash\vec{a}_t} & \Sigma_{\backslash\vec{a}_t\vec{a}_t} \\ \Sigma_{\vec{a}_t\backslash\vec{a}_t} & \Sigma_{\vec{a}\vec{a}} \end{bmatrix}. \tag{3.5}$$

The mean relevance scores and covariance matrix can then be updated for non-ranked documents using the formulae

$$\vec{r}_{\backslash\vec{a}_t} = \vec{r}_{\backslash\vec{a}_t} + \Sigma_{\backslash\vec{a}_t\vec{a}_t}\Sigma_{\vec{a}\vec{a}}^{-1}(\vec{o} - \vec{r}_{\vec{a}_t}) \tag{3.6}$$
$$\Sigma_{\backslash\vec{a}_t\backslash\vec{a}_t} = \Sigma_{\backslash\vec{a}_t\backslash\vec{a}_t} - \Sigma_{\backslash\vec{a}_t\vec{a}_t}\Sigma_{\vec{a}_t\vec{a}_t}^{-1}\Sigma_{\vec{a}_t\backslash\vec{a}_t} \tag{3.7}$$

and click observations $\vec{o}$. Thus, for given actions and observations, the functions above can be used to define a new conditional multivariate Gaussian distribution of the probability of relevance of the remaining documents, given as $R_{t+1} \sim \mathcal{N}(\vec{r}_{\backslash\vec{a}_t}, \Sigma_{\backslash\vec{a}_t\backslash\vec{a}_t}|\vec{a}_t, \vec{o})$.

When considering the objective from page t until page T, we use a weighted sum of the expected DCG@M scores of the rankings of the remaining result pages for the reward function, denoted here by

$$\mathcal{R}(\vec{a}_t, \vec{r}_t) = \lambda_t \sum_{i=1}^{M} \frac{\mathrm{E}[R_{a_{ti}}]}{\log_2\left(i + (t-1)M + 1\right)} \tag{3.8}$$

where $\mathrm{E}[R_{a_{ti}}] = \hat{r}_{ti}$ is the estimated relevance of the document chosen for rank position i on result page t. The overall utility across all pages is thus $\sum_{t=1}^{T} \mathcal{R}(\vec{a}_t, \vec{r}_t)$. The rank weight $\frac{1}{i+(t-1)M+1}$ is used to give greater weight to ranking the most relevant documents in higher positions and on earlier pages.

Before presenting a ranked list at result page 1 and directly observing $\vec{o}$, it remains an unknown variable and can be predicted using our prior knowledge. In order to perform exploration (active learning), we will need to be able to predict how a user will respond to each potential ranking. Using the model above, we can predict the user's feedback based on a particular rank action $\vec{a}$ by noting that $\vec{o}$ also follows the multivariate Gaussian distribution,

$$o_a \sim \mathcal{N}(\hat{r}_a, \hat{\sigma}_a). \tag{3.9}$$

In order to optimize over this statistical process, we use the Bellman Equation [24]. Let $V(\vec{r}_t, \Sigma_t, t)$ be the value function for maximizing the user satisfaction of the ranking up until step

T. Setting $t = 1$, we can derive the Bellman Equation as

$$V(\vec{\mathbf{r}}_1, \Sigma_1, 1) = \max_{\vec{\mathbf{a}}_1} \left[\lambda_1 \vec{\mathbf{r}}_1 \cdot \boldsymbol{W}_1 + \mathrm{E}\left[V(\vec{\mathbf{r}}_2, \Sigma_2, 2) \middle| \vec{\mathbf{o}} \right] \right] \qquad (3.10)$$

where $\boldsymbol{W}_t = \left\langle \frac{1}{\log_2(1+(t-1)M)}, \cdots, \frac{1}{\log_2(M+(t-1)M)} \right\rangle$ is the DCG weight vector. By explicitly setting $T = 2$ and λ as a mixture model parameter, Eq. (3.10) is simplified to the dynamic objective function

$$V(\vec{\mathbf{r}}_1, \Sigma_1, 1) = \max_{\vec{\mathbf{a}}_1} \left[\lambda \vec{\mathbf{r}}_1 \cdot \boldsymbol{W}_1 + \max_{\vec{\mathbf{a}}_2} \left[(1 - \lambda) \int_{\vec{\mathbf{o}}} \vec{\mathbf{r}}_2 \cdot \boldsymbol{W}_2 P(\vec{\mathbf{o}} | \vec{\mathbf{a}}_1, \vec{\mathbf{r}}_1) \mathrm{d}\vec{\mathbf{o}} \right] \right]. \qquad (3.11)$$

As with dynamic search, the Bellman Equation allows us to model multi-page search as a POMDP, in this case with a dynamic document variable. In this case, the document relevance is the hidden state, the belief is modeled using the multivariate Gaussian distribution, the click-throughs are the observations, and the actions available to the system are the different rankings of documents, and finally the utility function defines the reward.

3.2   MULTI-ARMED BANDITS

In this lecture, reinforcement learning techniques such as MDPs and POMDPs have been discussed as methods usable in dynamic IR settings. Another relevant formulation is the *Multi-Armed Bandit* (MAB) [195], a classic statistical resource allocation problem usually described using the analogy of a casino with multiple one-armed bandit slot machines. At each time step, a single machine (or *arm* in the literature) is chosen and a reward drawn from its hidden probability distribution. Meanwhile, the rewards for the other arms remain unknown. Each of the slot machines has a different probability distribution of rewards, and the objective is to find the optimal strategy for playing them in order to maximize the overall accumulated reward over some time horizon.

An analytical, Markovian solution was posited by Gittens in 1979 [88], defining for each one-armed bandit a scalar value known as the **Gittens Index**. This index value represented the expected reward for playing an arm until a termination step, and so for each time step, the arm with the highest Gittens index value was the arm chosen to play. The computational intractability of the calculation of the index has led to the development of tractable solutions that can guarantee asymptotic regret bounds [149].

Regret is the commonly used evaluative framework for multi-armed bandit algorithms, defined as the difference between the sum of rewards of the optimal sequence of arms vs. those chosen by the MAB algorithm. Here, the regret ρ is given by

$$\rho = T \left(\max_i r_i \right) - \sum_{t=1}^{T} \hat{r}_t \qquad (3.12)$$

where r_i is the reward of the i-th arm and $\hat{r}_t$ is the reward of the arm chosen at time t. In dynamic programming and other optimal control formulations, the objective is to maximize the value function over time, whereas here the goal is to minimize the regret, which represents the loss in potential value caused by choosing incorrectly.

The multi-armed bandit formulation can be likened to the Markov-based models described so far. Like a POMDP, one can consider the reward distribution of each arm as its hidden state, and so the belief state is the estimated expected value of the reward for that arm. The action in this case is which arm is chosen at each time step, and the reward (and observation) is what is observed from the chosen arm. A key distinction lies in the fact that the hidden distribution of each bandit does not change over time, that is, there is no transition probability function as the arms are independent and fixed. This simplification, as well as the adaptability of MAB algorithms to different scenario settings, makes MABs a versatile tool that are useful in DIR, in particular online learning to rank.

3.2.1   EXPLORATION VS. EXPLOITATION

A key characteristic of the MAB formulation, as well as some of the described information filtering and active learning approaches [135], is the balance between exploration and exploitation. In the context of multi-armed bandits, *exploration* refers to the investigation of the hidden distribution of each arm by strategically playing them to observe their reward. Conversely, once this distribution has been reliably determined then *exploitation* occurs, whereby the arm with the estimated highest reward is played.

The estimated reward is typically given by the maximum likelihood estimate

$$\bar{r}_i = \frac{1}{M_i} \sum_{m=1}^{M_i} r_{i,m} \qquad (3.13)$$

which is the average reward for arm i played M_i times ($M_i \leq T$). A naïve, purely exploitative algorithm would simply pick the arm with the highest $\bar{r}_i$ at each time step, but could never recover if it picked sub-optimally. The ϵ-greedy strategy addresses this by introducing a probability ϵ that at each time step a random arm is chosen, otherwise the best arm so far is chosen with probability $1 - \epsilon$. This solution has been demonstrated to be effective in simple scenarios although it is sensitive to the tuning of the parameter ϵ and the reward distributions of the arms [13].

A popular and effective alternative is the **UCB** index-based approach [5, 13]. Here, at time t, the arm with the highest index value

$$\bar{r}_i + \sqrt{\frac{2 \ln t}{M_i}} \qquad (3.14)$$

is played. This is the upper Chernoff-Hoeffding confidence interval bound for the estimated reward for probability $1 - \frac{1}{t}$ and the algorithm comes with a regret bound of $\frac{8M}{\Delta*} \ln t + 5M$, where

$\Delta*$ is the difference in reward between the optimal arm and the next best arm. As t increases, the upper confidence bound increases logarithmically for those arms not being played. Playing an arm (increasing M_i) causes a linear decrease in this bound. This extra term allows for the exploration of arms throughout the lifetime of the algorithm. Arms with a high average reward are more likely to be played and exploited, resulting in a lower upper confidence bound, allowing for inferior arms to occasionally be played.

The UCB algorithm is effective in cases where the arms are known to be stochastic and independent, although in real world scenarios this is not often the case. The worse-case setting for a multi-armed bandit is the *adversarial* setting, whereby an adversary can purposefully return arms with a low average reward if it has been deterministically chosen (such as by an index-based algorithm like UCB) [11]. To counteract this, stochastic algorithms such as *Exp3* (Exponential-weight for Exploration and Exploitation) choose an arm at random at each time step according to the probability distribution

$$p_k(t) = (1 - \gamma)\frac{w_k(t)}{\sum_{j=1}^{K} w_j(t)} + \frac{\gamma}{K} \tag{3.15}$$

where $w_k(t)$ is an arm-dependent weight adjusted by $w_k(t+1) = w_k(t)e^{\gamma r_{k,t}/K p_k(t)}$ if arm k was chosen at time t, and γ is a tune-able parameter balancing the effect of the weights [15]. It can be shown that under certain conditions and setting $\gamma = \min\left(1, \sqrt{\frac{K \log K}{(e-1)\Delta*}}\right)$ that the regret bound is $2.63\sqrt{\Delta* K \log K}$.

3.2.2   MULTI-ARMED BANDIT VARIATIONS

The multi-armed bandit literature is diverse and the methods described so far are simply the well-known algorithms that work under simple, well-understood problem settings. Different settings have been proposed that are more reflective of practical situations. For example, the multi-play setting has been widely researched for use in news recommendation [126] and signal allocation [148]. In these cases, k arms are chosen and played at each time step rather than a single arm. Other variations of the classic formulation include arms that are dependent on one another [184], arms with non-stationary reward distributions [26], arms that have some probability of not being active at each time step [141] or that have a limited lifespan before being removed from the set of arms [50].

An alternative approach that is important to online learning to rank is the *contextual bandit*. Here, each arm has a feature vector associated with it which is related to its reward distribution. Thus, a contextual MAB algorithm learns both the reward distributions for each arm and also a relevance model for the features. This allows for an improved learning rate, as the model can be used to estimate the reward for uncertain or unplayed (or new) arms, playing those anticipated to be effective based on their features. This has found application in news article and ad recommendation [126, 151].

Relevant to pairwise learning to rank is the *dueling bandit*. Here, absolute rewards from individual arms are no longer observable. Instead, pairs of arms are chosen at each time step, and the observed "reward" is the outcome of their comparison, i.e., which has the higher reward [271]. This formulation is useful in cases where there is no natural way of directly measuring rewards but comparisons can be measured. This is applicable to the online learning to rank scenario where a user's subjective perception of the relevance of documents is difficult to collect and interpret, but through interleaved experiments comparisons between ranking systems can be reliably made [272].

3.3   RELATED WORK

Through information filtering, we have discussed the topics of relevance feedback and active learning. Their combination naturally leads us to exploring work in reinforcement learning, whether it be its application to IF [216], or its use in identifying queries that require an update to its ranking due to changing relevance [177].

In particular, we covered the multi-armed bandit theory as it is well utilized in existing dynamic IR research such as news recommendation. The use of contextual bandits in this area is well reported, for instance, matching article extracted features to those of the user in order to personalize news stories over time [157], or the use of a multi-play bandit to recommend a set of news articles [126]. Other reinforcement learning approaches such as online logistic regression also feature in this area [3]. A related research area has been ad recommendation, where implicit feedback has been used to learn which sponsored search results to display to users [58], or which ads to display based on the context of the user browsing the web [160]. An MAB variant that models arms with a limited lifespan has been used to model advertisements so that they can be optimally displayed over their temporary contract with the advertising network [50].

Otherwise, the use of multi-armed bandits has largely been confined to the area of online learning to rank. Generally, the arms in this setting can either be the documents themselves or lists of documents, depending on the learning to rank approach undertaken. An optimal online learning to rank strategy will involve choosing documents for each user that either maximizes what can be learned about those documents (exploration), or else those that are relevant (exploitation). Relevance feedback from the user is then treated as the reward and used to update the learning to rank model over time [107, 222]. Regret in this scenario could be interpreted as the loss in user satisfaction over time compared to knowing the optimal ranking of documents in advance.

In pointwise online learning to rank, the relevance of each document is learned individually. One such approach has been to assign a multi-armed bandit to each rank position that learns the optimal document to display there [189]. A dependency between the bandits is introduced by the restriction that documents are chosen from the top rank onward and that documents can't be duplicated in the ranking. This dependency causes the algorithm to find an optimal and naturally diversified ranking over time. This approach was shown to be improved by incorporating the portfolio theory of IR [250] into an alternative UCB-style approach that ranked documents according to their index scores [227], resulting in a more efficient, optimally diverse ranking over time [226].

In listwise online learning to rank, a dueling bandit is used to compare two lists of search results [272]. Another approach has been to use stochastic gradient descent and probabilistic interleaving to compare ranking lists over time [108]. In this case, the implicit feedback is carefully interpreted using different click models and the degree of exploration and exploitation finely tuned. Generally, listwise comparison is usually made by interleaving the lists and using implicit feedback to evaluate which is better, and can be accomplished using a range of techniques [188, 215].

CHAPTER 4

Dynamic IR for Sessions

Search is often triggered by a task. To accomplish the search task, search queries rarely happen independent of each other; instead, they often appear in a session that consists of multiple iterations of searches that depend on each other, and the session develops as time goes by. As a dynamic procedure with many user interactions and changes in the process, session search is an important topic in Dynamic IR studies. A session starts when a user issues a query, which is often unclear or under-specified in the first instance, and the search system retrieves a ranked list of relevant documents. After examining the document titles and snippets, a user may click on some of the webpages. The user's cognitive focus and understanding of the information need may change as they gain information from the documents. The next interaction occurs when the user *reformulates* their query, retrieving a new ranked list of documents. We term the process from one query formulation to the next query formulation a **search iteration**. A search session consists of several **query reformulations** that reflect the user's shifting cognitive focus and understanding of their information need, and stops when they are satisfied or become frustrated or bored [56].

Understanding the dynamic user behavior that occurs during session search has been a topic of interest in IR research in recent years. The intentions of users during exploratory searches [47], learning when session search personalization is useful [242] and how the relevance of previous documents affects ranking quality [95] are all examples of current research in the area. In a search session, the user explores the information space by inputting queries, examining retrieved documents and clicking on those that seem relevant. In support of this, between 2010 and 2014, TREC organized a series of tracks with associated session-based search logs that encouraged research in this area [131, 132]. An example session search from the TREC 2013 session track dataset is given in Table 1.1.

In a session, each query reformulation usually acts as an advancement of the user satisfying their information need, yet we often observe unexpected changes in queries and the user's search intent. We can attribute these changes to two opposing explanations: the user is satisfied with the search results and moves on to another subtopic information need; or the user is unsatisfied with the search results and abandons the previous search path. The complexity in understanding this type of decision making makes session search challenging.

4.1 SESSION SEARCH

Session search is an Information Retrieval (IR) task which extends classic ad-hoc retrieval by handling more than one query in a retrieval task. This form of search happens everyday when people search online using a series of queries for a complex information need, such as planning a trip to Paris or purchasing a new home. The process of submitting multiple queries in a session to accomplish a complex information need is called *session search*.

A session usually starts with the user issuing a query to the search engine. The user then receives a list of ranked documents that are ordered by the decreasing relevance to the query. The user then goes through the list and skims the snippets, clicks on some interesting ones and spends a fair amount of time reading them. This is a complete cycle of an ad-hoc retrieval process. Here in session search, we call one such information retrieval cycle a "search iteration" and it repeats in the session. In the next search iteration, the user either reformulates the previous query or writes a new one to start another search. The loop stops when the user's information need is satisfied or the user abandons the search. As a result, there are a series of search iterations in a session—which include a series of queries $q_1, ..., q_n$, a series of returned documents $D_1, ..., D_n$, and a series of clicks $C_1, ..., C_n$, some of which are examined by the user for a long time and thus potentially highly relevant documents (They are called SAT-clicks, or *satisfactory clicked documents* [85]).

Session search has obtained increasing attentions in the IR community, for instance, in the recent dynamic information retrieval modeling approaches [164, 165, 261, 262] and in the TExt Retrieval Conference (TREC) 2010–2014 Session Tracks [132, 133]. The current approaches include (1) extending existing IR techniques, such as learning to rank and using large scale query logs, from ad-hoc retrieval for one-shot query to session search, and (2) emerging efforts in applying reinforcement learning (RL) to session search.

It is often puzzling what drives a user's search in a session and why they make certain moves. We observe that sometimes the same user behavior, such as a drift from one subtopic to another, can be explained by opposite reasons: either the user is satisfied with the search results and moves to another sub information need, or the user is not satisfied with the search results and leaves the previous search path. The complexity of users' decision-making patterns makes session search quite challenging [47, 242].

Researchers have attempted to find out the causes of topic drifting in session search. The causes under study include personalization [242], task types [131, 162] and previous documents' relevance [95]. A user study is usually needed to draw conclusions about user intent. However, the focus of Dynamic IR for sessions is not on identifying user intent. Instead, the focus is on developing frameworks that are able to capture the dynamics in the entire search process and effectively retrieve documents that satisfy the long-term information need in the entire session.

In the recent developed Dynamic IR models for sessions, there are a few interesting phenomenons being made in session search. These phenomenons provide good intuitions for modeling the complex process in session search. These interesting phenomenons include query changes, the Markov chains in sessions and the two-communication between the user and the search engine in sessions.

Table 4.1: Examples of TREC 2012 Session queries

session 6	session 28
1. pocono mountains pennsylvania	1. france world cup 98
2. pocono mountains pennsylvania hotels	reaction stock market
3. pocono mountains pennsylvania things to do	2. france world cup 98
4. pocono mountains pennsylvania hotels	reaction
5. pocono mountains camelbeach	3. france world cup 98
6. pocono mountains camelbeach hotel	
7. pocono mountains chateau resort	session 32
8. pocono mountains chateau resort attractions	1. bollywood legislation
9. pocono mountains chateau resort getting to	2. bollywood law
10. chateau resort getting to	
11. pocono mountains chateau resort directions	
session 85	session 37
1. glass blowing	1. Merck lobbyists
2. glass blowing science	2. Merck lobbying U.S.
3. scientific glass blowing	policy

4.1.1 QUERY CHANGE: A STRONG SIGNAL FROM THE USER

In a session, we often observe that the queries change constantly. As shown in Table 4.1, the patterns of query changes include general to specific (*pocono mountains pennsylvania → pocono mountains pennsylvania hotels*), specific to general (*france world cup 98 reaction → france world cup 98*), drifting from one to another (*pocono mountains pennsylvania hotels → pocono mountains camelbeach*), or slightly different expressions for the same information need (*glass blowing science → scientific glass blowing*). These changes vary and sometimes even look random (*gun homicides australia → martin bryant port arthur massacre*), which increases the difficulty of understanding user intention. However, since query changes are made after the user examines search results, it is believed that *query change is an important form of feedback*. Query changes have been used as one of the major types of user actions or feedback in session search. As mentioned in [94], query change might be an even stronger signal of user intent than clicks and dwell time.

It is difficult to interpret the user intent [46, 242] behind query change. For instance, for a query change from *Kurosawa* to *Kurosawa wife* (s38), there is no indication about "wife" in the search results returned for the first query. However, *Kurosawa's wife* is actually among the information needs in the topic descriptions provided to the user by TREC organizers. Our experience with TREC Session tracks suggests that information needs and previous search results are two main factors that influence query change. However, knowing information needs before search

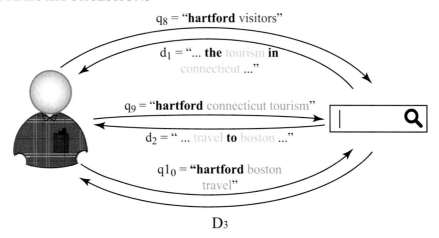

Figure 4.1: Examples of query changes during session search, in this case, queries 8, 9 and 10 in the example session in Table 1.1. In this case, the user has removed the term "*visitors*" from q_8 (indicated in red) and replaced it with the terms "*tourism*" and "*connecticut*" discovered in document d_1 (given in yellow), creating the new query q_9 (new terms given in green). A similar process occurs for the next query.

could not easily be achieved. This paper focuses on utilizing evidence found in previous search results and the relationship between previous search results and query change to improve session search.

Query change Δq_t is defined as the syntactic editing changes between two adjacent queries q_{t-1} and q_t:

$$\Delta q_t = q_t - q_{t-1}$$

q_t can be written as a combination of the shared portion between q_t and q_{t-1} and the query change $q_t = (q_t \cap q_{t-1}) + \Delta q_t$.

The query change Δq_t comes from two sources. First, the added terms, which can be called *positive Δq*, which are new terms that the user adds to the previous query. Second, the removed terms, which can be called *negative Δq*, which are terms that the user deletes from the previous query. The common terms shared by two adjacent queries are called *theme terms* since they often represent the main topic of a session.

The query change terms can be grouped into three sources:

- Theme terms (q_{theme}) are terms that appear in both q_{t-1} and q_t. In fact, they often appear in many queries in a session. This implies a strong preference for those terms from the user. If they appear in D_{t-1}, it shows that the user favors them since the user issues them again

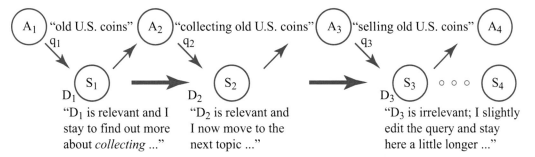

Figure 4.2: A Markov chain of decision-making states in session search. (S: decision-making states; q: queries; A: user actions such as query changes; D: documents).

in q_t. If they do not appear in D_{t-1}, the user still favors them due to their inclusion in the next query.

- Added terms $(+\Delta q)$ are terms that appear only in q_t, not in q_{t-1}. They indicate specification, a destination of topic drifting, or the result of a slight change in topic. If they appear in D_{t-1}, for the sake of novelty [118], they will not be favored in D_t. If they do not appear in D_{t-1}, this means that they are novel and the user now favors them.

- Removed terms $(-\Delta q)$ are terms that appear only in q_{t-1}, not in q_t. They indicate generalization, the start of topic drifting and the source of slight changes. If they appear in D_{t-1}, removing them means that the user observes them and dislikes them. If they do not appear in D_{t-1}, the user still dislikes the terms since they are not in q_t anyway.

4.1.2   MARKOV CHAINS IN SESSIONS

Another interesting phenomenon in session search is a Markov chain within it—a user's judgment of retrieved documents in the previous search iteration affects a user's actions in the next iteration. Figure 4.2 illustrates TREC 2013 Session Track session 9. The user started with the first query "old US coins" and received a list of documents returned by the search engine as D_1. The user examined the documents and thought: "This set of documents look relevant and I would like to find out more about a more specific aspect of the current query." So the user issued the next query on "collecting old US coins," which is one of the subtopics about "old US coins." Again the user got a list of documents from the search engine, and this time she thought "D_2 looks relevant too. I am happy. Now I am ready to move to the next subtopic." Then the user wrote another query about a different subtopic, which is "selling old US coins." So the user liked the retrieval results but still decided to move to other topics. In the next search iteration, the user found that "D_3 is not relevant. It might be some problem with my query. So I would slightly edit my query and try to investigate this subtopic a little longer." Then the search goes on.

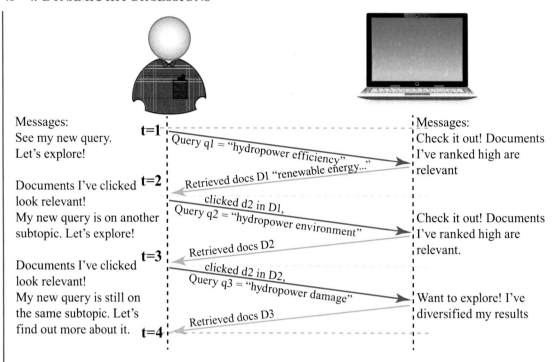

Figure 4.3: Interactions in session search. (Example is from TREC'14 Session 52. d_n is the nth document in a ranked list D at iteration t.)

We observe a Markov chain of query and document changes in the process: what the user sees and reads in the previous search iteration(s) has an impact on her next query. A Markov chain is a memoryless random process where the next state depends only on the current state [124]. In the session, a user's judgment of the retrieved documents in the previous iteration affects or even decides the user's actions in the next iteration. A user's actions could include clicks, query changes, reading the documents, etc. The user's gain, which we call *reward*, is the amount of relevant information that he or she obtains in the retrieved documents. The reward then motivates the later user actions in the subsequent search iterations.

In fact, not only the user, but also the search engine, makes decisions in a Markov process. A search engine takes in a user's feedback and improves its retrieval algorithm iteration after iteration to achieve a better reward too. The search engine actions could include term weighting, turning on or turning off one or more of its search techniques, or adjusting parameters for the techniques. For instance, based on the reward, the search engine can select p in deciding the top p documents used in pseudo relevance feedback.

4.1.3   TWO-WAY COMMUNICATION IN SESSIONS

There are rich user and search engine interactions that occur during session search. We believe that they are valuable resources and we should take advantage of them to improve search results' effectiveness. For instance, Figure 4.3 illustrates the interactions and the messaging between the user and the search engine in a session. The example is taken from TREC 2014 Session 52, which searches for *the efficiency, technology and environment effect of hydropower*. At iteration 1 ($t = 1$), the user enters the first query, "hydropower efficiency."[1] The search engine sends out its ranked documents D_1 as its message. At iteration 2 ($t = 2$), the user sends out the browsing information, including clicked documents (some of them are SAT-clicked[2]) and time spent on those documents, and then sends out a reformulated query q_2. Both the browsing information and the query reformulations are messages (feedback) that the user sends to the search engine. The search engine then sends out a new set of documents D_2 for this iteration. At $t = 3$, the user again sends out the browsing information and the reformulated query q_3, and the search engine replies with D_3. The loop continues until the search is done.

Session search has been viewed as a cooperative game played between the user and the search engine in recent work [164, 169]. The interactions between the two agents show the following characteristics:

Common goal.   The two parties (agents) in session search, the user and the search engine, share a common goal, which is to find documents that can satisfy the ultimate information need. Throughout the process, the two agents cooperate and explore together, seeking a better understanding of the information need and how to satisfy it by finding relevant documents.

Exploration in the unknown information space.   The user and the search engine interact in a complex search system to realize a goal: satisfying an ultimate information need. The search process is guided by a hidden, complex, sometimes vague information need, which is always in the user's mind, and may evolve and become clearer as the search develops. The user and the search engine work together step by step, exploring an unknown information space, to find the relevant documents to satisfy the information need. Within the process, a search iteration could be generalization, specification, slight change or complete change to the previous query. All these search attempts from the user accumulate knowledge and information that allow the user to better understand the ultimate search goal, and the change and dynamics presented in the search process.

Equal partners.   Both the user and the search engine are viewed as autonomous agents who are *equal partners* in their cooperation. Our view is different from prior work on interactive search where the users are the only main target in the study. Hence, the roles of the user and the search engine are not that one is teaching and another is learning. Instead, in a joint exploration, neither of them may have a clear picture of how to approach the information need. Sometimes neither

---

[1]There has not yet been clicking or browsing at iteration 1.
[2]In this book, we consider a document with dwell time longer than 30 seconds as satisfactory clicks (SAT-clicks).

Table 4.2: Message interpretations

Messages	"These are relevant!"	"Let's explore!"
User:	"Hey, after reading the documents, those documents that I have clicked or SAT-clicked are potentially relevant. Please pay attention to those documents that I have clicked"	"I have written a query that *shifts* to new topics. I would like us to explore some new topics together."
Search Engine:	"Hello, the documents that I've ranked high for you are supposed to be relevant. The more relevant I think they are, the higher that I rank them. Please take a look."	"I have a method to recommend novel documents to you as well. When I do it, I introduce some documents on new topics to increase *diversity*. Please take a look at those documents that I bring to the top positions in the ranking list but may seem not directly related to your current query; they are what I recommend on new topics and hope we both explore them."

of them knows how to describe the information need. For instance, the user may have difficulty articulating a query that precisely describes the information need, especially when the search task is complex. Therefore, we would like to point out that both parties are equal, and that they take turns in exploring the environment and communicating with each other to reach the goal.

Cooperative exploration.   Both the user and the search engine can make decisions on relevance, as well as on when and where to explore the information space. A user can issue a new query from one subtopic to another. This drift drives the search process into a new direction. Similarly, the search engine can also drive the search process into new paths, by introducing diversity in the search results that it recommends. In our opinion, both agents are not only able to tell each other what documents they find to be relevant from their own points of view, but are also able to suggest to each other new directions for exploration.

Both the user and the search engine communicate and act using these messages. Table 4.2 shows an interpretation of their messages. Based on this intuition, researchers [164] have modeled the two-way feedback between the user and the search engine to facilitate session search. Basically, the two agents use *documents* and other actions, such as queries, to express their opinions on two things: (1) which documents are *relevant* and (2) whether they would like to inform the other party to *explore* other subtopics as a team. That is to say, there is a two-way feedback mechanism in which the user and the search engine talk to each other every time when they communicate—*whether*

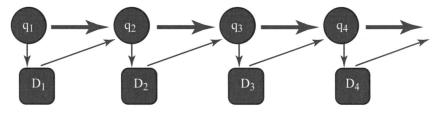

Figure 4.4: Query states in a session.

an agent judges the previously retrieved/recommended documents by the other agent are relevant and *whether an agent would like to lead both of them to explore and move to the next sub information need.*

4.2   MODELING SESSIONS IN THE DYNAMIC IR FRAMEWORK

A Dynamic IR system is made up of states, actions, rewards and a state transition function which determines how the state of the dynamic agent changes over time. The goal in a Dynamic IR system is to find an optimal policy $\pi(s) = a$ that dictates which action to take given the state of the agent. We can liken this to session search by supposing that the query in each impression is the state that the agent (the search system) is in. This section describes the design options that a session-based Dynamic IR system could take.

4.2.1   STATES

In the most natural way of modeling states in a session, the states could be the queries themselves (as shown in Figure 4.4). A state transition model can be used to specify how queries change throughout a search session. In this case, the actions available to the search system are to adjust the term weights or relevance scores of documents. In the case of the user, the actions available to them are to add, remove or retain terms from query to query. Here, the optimal policy represents the best ranking of documents for each query in the search session.

Session search can also be modeled with hidden states, representing the unobservable underlying information need of the user. In this case, a POMDP is the more appropriate model to use. For instance, inspired by earlier research on user intent and task types [162, 240], Luo et al. [169] proposed four hidden decision making states for session search. They are identified based on two dimensions: (1) "relevant dimension"—whether the user thinks the returned documents are relevant, and (2) "exploration dimension"—whether the user would like to explore another subtopic. The two dimensions greatly simplify the complexity of user modeling in session search. The relatively small number of discrete states enables us to proceed with POMDP and its opti-

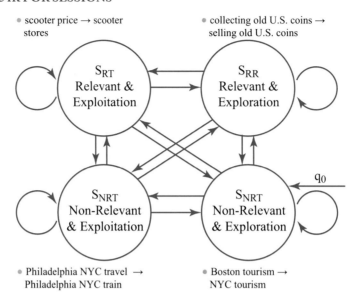

Figure 4.5: Users' decision-making states in a session.

mization at low cost. The cross-product of the two dimensions results in four states: (i) user finds a relevant document from the returned documents and decides to explore the next sub information need (relevant and exploration, e.g., *scooter price → scooter stores*), (ii) user finds relevant information and decides to stay in the current sub information need to look into more relevant information (relevant and exploitation, e.g., *hartford visitors → hartford connecticut tourism*), (iii) user finds out that the returned documents are not relevant and decides to stay and try out different expressions for the same sub information need (non-relevant and exploitation, e.g., *philadelphia nyc travel → philadelphia nyc train*), (iv) user finds out that documents are not relevant and decides to give up and move on to another sub information need (non-relevant and exploration, e.g., *distance new york boston → maps.bing.com*).

Figure 4.5 shows the decision state diagram for Dynamic IR models. The subscriptions stand for {$RT = RelevantexploiTation$, $RR = RelevantexploRation$, $NRT = NonRelevantexploiTation$, $NRR = NonRelevantexploRation$}. We insert a dummy starting query q_0 before any real query and it always goes to S_{NRR}. The series of search iterations in a session move in the decision-making states from one to the next. A sequence of states can be time stamped and presented as $s_t = S_m$, where $t = 1, 2, ..., n$ and $m = \{RT, RR, NRT, NRR\}$.

The definition of the states is essential for modeling in IR. Related research in similar tasks have proposed a variety of state definitions, including *queries* [95, 108], *document relevance* [120, 277] and *decision making* [169]. We group the setting of states into two design options:

Fixed number of states   A predefined, fixed number of states can help to easily characterize certain properties of the session based on the current state. For instance, Zhang et al. [277] used two binary relevance states, "Relevant" and "Irrelevant," to represent the decision-making states that the user agent can consider for retrieved documents. The dual-agent example above is a more comprehensive example where four states are considered [169].

Varying number of states   Some approaches choose to model session search using a varying or even infinite number of states. A popular approach is to model queries in a session as states (Guan et al. [95]). In this design, the number of states changes according to session length, i.e., the number of queries in a session. There are also abstract definitions of states, for instance, Jin et al. [120] used a continuous relevance score distribution for the states, which leads to an infinite number of real valued states.

The state definitions are used to characterize the current status of the search process. Using a fixed number of states tends to reflect more specific features while using a varying number of states leads to a more abstract characterization of the search process. It is worth pointing out that *state definition is an art*, which depends on the needs of the actual IR task and the design of the system and model.

4.2.2   ACTIONS

Actions by Agents

Actions can be grouped from the perspective of who did the action, the user or the search engine. For session search, typical user actions include: adding/removing/retaining query terms, clicking on documents and document dwell time. Typical search engine actions include: increasing/decreasing/keeping term weights, query expansion, adjusting the number of top documents used in pseudo relevance feedback and the choice of the ranked list of documents itself. Here we focus on the search engine actions, which can be grouped into:

Algorithm Selection   Some approaches use a meta-level modeling of actions. They don't focus on details in a single search method but on implementing multiple search methods (termed as *search algorithms*), and selecting the best search technology to use. An action using technology selection can be *switching on or switching off the algorithm*, or *adjusting parameters in the algorithm*. Example technologies include query expansion and pseudo relevance feedback. To illustrate, Luo et al. [169] selected the number of top retrieved documents to be included in pseudo relevance feedback.

Term Weight Adjustments   Another method is to adjust term weights. Typical weighting schemes include *increasing term weights, decreasing term weights* or *keeping term weights unchanged*. Guan et al. [95] proposed four types of term weighting scheme (*theme terms, novel added terms, previously retrieved added terms* and *removed terms*) as actions according to the query changes detected between adjacent search iterations.

Portfolio   A more straightforward type of search engine action is the document ranking list which we call *portfolio* selection [226]. Here a ranked list of documents is a *portfolio* and is treated as a single action. The space of the document permutation is the action space, where each document ranking permutation is a different action.

Actions by Scope

Actions can also be grouped from the perspective of its scope, within the two agents or between the two and the environment. There are thus two levels of actions in the Dynamic IR modeling of session search. They are domain-level actions and communications-level actions. Both the user and the search engine agents have actions at these two levels.

Domain-level Actions   The domain-level actions represent the actions directly performed on the world (document collection) by the user agent and by the search engine agent, respectively. The common user actions include *writing a query, clicking a document, SAT-clicking a document, reading a snippet, reading a document, changing a query* and *eye-tracking the documents*. Common user actions include query changes and clicks. However, the Dynamic IR formulation can be easily adopted for other types of user actions. The search engine domain-level actions A_{se} include increasing, decreasing and maintaining the term weights, as well as adjusting parameters in one or more search techniques.

Communications-level Actions (Messages)   The second level of actions are communication-level actions (messages). They are actions only performed between agents. These messages are essentially used to model what *documents* an agent thinks are relevant. User messages are the set of documents (being clicked) that the user sends out. They are defined as the clicked documents $D_{clicked}$. In TREC 2013 Session, 31% of search iterations contain SAT-clicked documents; 23.9% of sessions contain 1 to 4 SAT-clicked documents; and a few sessions, for instance Sessions 45, 57 and 72, contain around 10 SAT-clicked documents; 88.7% of SAT-clicked documents appear in the top 10 retrieved results.

Similarly, search engine messages are the set of documents that the search engine sends out. They are the top k returned documents (k ranges from 0 to 55 in the TREC setting). They demonstrate what documents the search engine thinks are the most relevant. In TREC 2013, 2.8% (10) search iterations return fewer than 10 documents, 90.7% (322) return exactly 10, 5.1% (18) return 10~20, and 1.4% (5) return 20~55 documents.

4.2.3   REWARDS

In a Dynamic IR system, each state is associated with a *reward function* $\mathcal{R}$ that indicates possible positive reward or negative loss that may result for a state and an action. In order to estimate the benefits from an action, we need to evaluate the reward of taking the action at state s. Similar to the loss (risk) function in supervised learning, a reward function guides the search system throughout the entire dynamic process of session search. Since session search is a document retrieval task, it's natural that the reward function is related to the document relevance. Notably, the difference between session search and adhoc query search lies in that session search aims to optimize a *long-term reward*, which is an expectation over the overall rewards in the whole session, while adhoc retrieval only optimizes for an individual query. In [167], reward functions in a Dynamic IR system can be grouped into:

Explicit Rewards.   Rewards directly generated from a user's relevance assessments are considered as explicit feedback. Both Jin et al. [120] and Luo et al. [169] calculated the rewards using nDCG, which measures the document relevance for an entire ranked list of documents with ground truth judgments.

Implicit Rewards.   Other approaches used implicit feedback obtained from user behavior as rewards. For instance, Hofmann et al. [108] used user click information as the reward function in their online learning to ranking algorithm and Zhang et al. [277] used clicks and dwell time as a reward for document re-ranking.

4.3 DUAL-AGENT STOCHASTIC GAME: PUTTING USERS INTO RETRIEVAL MODELS

The dynamics in session search, including decision-making states, query changes, clicks and rewards, can be mathematically modeled as a cooperative stochastic game played between the user and the search engine. When there is more than one agent in a POMDP, the POMDP becomes a stochastic game (SG). The two agents in session search are the user agent and the search engine agent. In contrast to most two-player scenarios, such as chess games in game theory, the two agents in session search are not opponents to each other; instead, they cooperate: they share the decision states and work together to jointly maximize their goals. Luo et al. [169] termed their framework "**win-win search**" for its efforts in ensuring that both agents arrive at a win-win situation. One may argue that in reality a commercial search engine and a user may have different goals and that is why some commercial search engines put their sponsors high in the returned results.

4.3.1 FRAMEWORK FORMULATION

A dual-agent stochastic game (SG) can be represented as a tuple $< S, A_u, A_{se}, \Sigma_u, \Sigma_{se}, \Omega_u, \Omega_{se}, O, B, T, R >$. Table 4.3 lists the symbols and their meanings in the dual-agent SG. S is the decision-making states that we mentioned in Section 4.2.1. A_u, A_{se}, Σ_u and Σ_{se} are the actions. The actions are divided into two types: domain-level actions A, what an agent acts on the world directly, and communication-level actions Σ, also known as *messages*, which only go between the agents. User actions A_u are mainly query changes [95] while search engine actions A_{se} are term weighting schemes and adjustments to search techniques. Both Σ_u and Σ_{se} are sets of relevant documents that an agent uses to inform the other agent

Table 4.3: Symbols in the dual-agent stochastic game

Name	Symbol	Meanings
State	S	the four hidden decision-making states
User action	A_u	add query terms, remove query terms, keep query terms
Search engine action	A_{se}	increase/decrease/keep term weights, adjust search techniques, etc.
Message from user to search engine	Σ_u	clicked and SAT-clicked documents
Message from search engine to user	Σ_{se}	top k returned documents
User's observation	Ω_u	observations that the user makes from the world
Search engine's observation	Ω_{se}	observations that the search engine makes from the world and from the user
User reward	R_u	relevant information the user gains from reading the documents
Search engine reward	R_{se}	nDCG that the search gains by returning documents
Belief state	B	belief states generated from the belief updater and shared by both agents

about what they consider as relevant. (Section 4.2.2) Ω is the observation that an agent can draw from the world or from the other agent. O is the observation function that maps states and actions to observations: $O : S \times A \rightarrow \Omega$ or $O : S \times \Sigma \rightarrow \Omega$. Note that the actions can be domain-level actions A or messages Σ, or a combination of both (Sec. 4.3.2). B is the set of belief states shared by both agents. The beliefs are updated every time when an observation happens. There are two types of belief: $B_{\bullet\Sigma}$, beliefs before the messages and $B_{\Sigma\bullet}$, beliefs after the messages. The reward function R is defined over $B \times A \rightarrow \mathbb{R}$. It is the amount of document relevance that an agent obtains from the world. R_{se} is the nDCG score (normalized Discounted Cumulative Gain [131]) that the search engine gains for the documents it returns. R_u is the relevance that the user gains from reading the documents.

The two agents share the decision-making states and beliefs but differ in actions, messages and policies. Although they also make different observations, both contribute to the belief updater; the difference is thus absorbed. As a retrieval model, Dynamic IR pays more attention to the search engine policy $\pi_{se} : B \rightarrow A$.

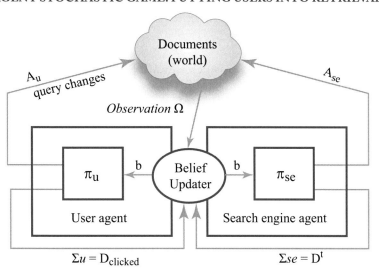

Figure 4.6: Dual-agent stochastic game.

The Stochastic Game

Figure 4.6 further illustrates the model. The stochastic game is carried out by following the steps below:

1. At search iteration $t = 0$, both agents begin in the same initial state S^0.

2. t increases by one: $t = t + 1$. The user agent writes a query q^t and takes the tth user agent action a_u^t, which is a query change from the previous query.

3. (*) The search engine agent makes observations Ω_{se} from the world and updates its before-message-belief-state $b_{\bullet\Sigma se}^t$ based on $O(S^t, a_u^t, \Omega_{se})$.

4. The search engine runs its optimization algorithm and picks the best policy π_{se}, which maximizes the joint long term rewards for both agents. Following the policy, it takes actions a_{se}^t. This is where the model performs retrieval.

5. Search engine action a_{se}^t results in a set of documents D^t, which are returned as message Σ_{se}^t sent from the search engine agent to the user agent through the world.

6. (*) The user agent receives message Σ_{se}^t and observes Ω_u. If the user would like to stop the search, the process ends. Otherwise, the user updates the after-message-belief-state $b_{\Sigma\bullet u}^t$ based on $O(S^t, \Sigma_{se}^t, \Omega_u)$.

7. Based on the current beliefs, the user agent sends its feedback messages Σ_u^t to inform the search engine agent. Σ_u^t are clicks, some of which are SAT-clicks. It contains a set of documents $D_{clicked}$.

8. (*) The search engine agent observes Ω_{se} from the world and updates its after-message-belief-state $b^t_{\Sigma \bullet se}$ based on $O(S^t, \Sigma^t_u, \Omega_{se})$.

9. The user agent picks a policy π_u, which is not the interest in this book, and continues to send out actions a^{t+1}_u in the form of query changes. The world moves into a new state s_{t+1}. $t = t + 1$. The process repeats from step 3.

Steps 3, 6 and 8 happen after making an observation from the world or from the other agent. They then all involve a belief update.

4.3.2   OBSERVATION FUNCTIONS

In the stochastic game between the user and the search engine agents, at three steps, the agents make observations and update the belief states. The steps are: Steps 3 and 8 are search engine observations, and step 6 is user observation. Both observations on the user and on the search engine can be used to jointly update the beliefs. Therefore, instead of three, two types of observations can be made. Here we show how to calculate the observation functions.

The observation function $O(s_j, a_t, \omega_t)$, defined as $P(\omega_t | s_j, a_t)$, is the probability of observing $\omega_t \in \Omega$ when agents take action a_t and land on state s_j. The first type of observation is related to *relevance*. In the stochastic game's Step 8, after the user sends the message Σ_u (user clicks) out at Step 7, the search engine updates its after-message-belief-state $b_{\Sigma \bullet se}$ based on its observation of user clicks. The observation function for "Relevant" states is:

$$O(s_t=\text{Rel}, \Sigma_u, \omega_t=\text{Rel}) \overset{def}{=\!=\!=} P(\omega_t = \text{Rel} | s_t = \text{Rel}, \Sigma_u). \tag{4.1}$$

It can be written as $\frac{P(\omega_t=\text{Rel}, s_t=\text{Rel}, \Sigma_u)}{P(s_t=\text{Rel}, \Sigma_u)}$. By taking $P(s_t = \text{Rel}, \Sigma_u)$ as a constant, which can be approximated by $P(\omega_t = \text{Rel}, s_t = \text{Rel}, \Sigma_u) = P(s_t = \text{Rel} | \omega_t = \text{Rel}, \Sigma_u) P(\omega_t = \text{Rel}, \Sigma_u)$. Given that user clicks Σ_u are highly correlated to ω_t, which can be approximated as $P(s_t = \text{Rel} | \omega_t = \text{Rel}, \Sigma_u)$ by $P(s_t = \text{Rel} | \omega_t = \text{Rel})$. Further, by taking $P(\Sigma)$ as a constant, it becomes

$$\begin{aligned} O(s_t=\text{Rel}, \Sigma_u, \omega_t=\text{Rel}) &\propto P(s_t = \text{Rel} | \omega_t = \text{Rel}) P(\omega_t = \text{Rel}, \Sigma_u) \\ &\propto P(s_t = \text{Rel} | \omega_t = \text{Rel}) P(\omega_t = \text{Rel} | \Sigma_u). \end{aligned} \tag{4.2}$$

Similarly, it becomes

$$\begin{aligned} O(s_t=&\text{Non-Rel}, \Sigma_u, \omega_t=\text{Non-Rel}) \\ &\propto P(s_t = \text{Non-Rel} | \omega_t = \text{Non-Rel}) P(\omega_t = \text{Non-Rel} | \Sigma_u) \end{aligned} \tag{4.3}$$

as well as $O(s_t=\text{Non-Rel}, \Sigma_u, \omega_t=\text{Rel})$ and $O(s_t=\text{Rel}, \Sigma_u, \omega_t=\text{Non-Rel})$.

Based on whether a SAT-click exists or not, we can calculate the probability of the SG landing at the "Relevant" states or the "Non-Relevant" states (the first dimension of hidden decision-making states). At search iteration t, if the set of previously returned documents leads to one or more SAT-clicks, the current state is likely to be relevant, otherwise non-relevant. That is to say,

$$s_t \text{ is likely to be } \begin{cases} \text{Relevant} & \text{if } \exists\, d \in D_{t-1} \text{ and} \\ & d \text{ is SAT-clicked} \\ \text{Non-Relevant} & \text{otherwise.} \end{cases} \tag{4.4}$$

Based on this intuition, it is calculated as $P(\omega_t = \text{Rel}|\Sigma_u)$ and $P(\omega_t = \text{Non-Rel}|\Sigma_u)$ as:

$$P(\omega_t = \text{Rel}|\Sigma_u) = P(\exists\, \text{SATClicks} \in D^{t-1}_{clicked}) \tag{4.5}$$

$$P(\omega_t = \text{Non-Rel}|\Sigma_u) = P(\nexists\, \text{SATClicks} \in D^{t-1}_{clicked}). \tag{4.6}$$

The second type of observation is related to *exploitation vs. exploration*. This corresponds to a combined observation at Step 3 and the previous Step 6 in the stochastic game, where the SG update the before-message-belief-state $b_{\bullet\Sigma_{se}}$ for a user action a_u (query change) and a search engine message $\Sigma_{se}=D_{t-1}$, the top returned documents at the previous iteration. The search engine agent makes observations about exploitation vs. exploration (the second dimension of hidden decision-making states) by:

$$O(s_t=\text{Exploitation}, a_u=\Delta q_t, \Sigma_{se}=D_{t-1}, \omega_t=\text{Exploitation})$$
$$\propto P(s_t = \text{Exploitation}|\omega_t = \text{Exploitation})$$
$$\times P(\omega_t = \text{Exploitation}|\Delta q_t, D_{t-1}) \tag{4.7}$$

$$O(s_t=\text{Exploration}, a_u=\Delta q_t, \Sigma_{se}=D_{t-1}, \omega_t=\text{Exploration})$$
$$\propto P(s_t = \text{Exploration}|\omega_t = \text{Exploration})$$
$$\times P(\omega_t = \text{Exploration}|\Delta q_t, D_{t-1}). \tag{4.8}$$

The search engine can guess the hidden states based on the following intuition:

$$s_t \text{ is likely to be } \begin{cases} \text{Exploration} & \text{if } (+\Delta q_t \neq \emptyset \text{ and } +\Delta q_t \notin D_{t-1}) \\ & \text{or } (+\Delta q_t = \emptyset \text{ and } -\Delta q_t \neq \emptyset) \\ \text{Exploitation} & \text{if } (+\Delta q_t \neq \emptyset \text{ and } +\Delta q_t \in D_{t-1}) \\ & \text{or } (+\Delta q_t = \emptyset \text{ and } -\Delta q_t = \emptyset). \end{cases} \tag{4.9}$$

The idea is that given that D_{t-1} is the message from search engine and $a_u = \Delta q$ is the message from user, if added query terms $+\Delta q$ appear in D_{t-1}, it is likely that the user stays at the same sub information need from iteration $t - 1$ to t for "exploitation." On the other hand, if the added terms $+\Delta q$ do not appear in D_{t-1}, it is likely that the user moves to the next sub information need from iteration $t - 1$ to t for "exploration." In addition, if there are no added terms ($+\Delta q_t$ is empty) but there are deleted terms ($-\Delta q_t$ is not empty), it is likely that the user goes to a broader topic to explore. If $+\Delta q_t$ and $-\Delta q_t$ are both empty, it means there is no change to the query, it is likely to fall into exploitation.

Hence, $P(\omega_t|\Delta q_t, D_{t-1})$ can be calculated as:

$$P(\omega_t = \text{Exploration}|\Delta q_t, D_{t-1}) = \begin{aligned} & P(+\Delta q_t \neq \emptyset \wedge +\Delta q_t \notin D_{t-1}) \\ & + P(+\Delta q_t = \emptyset \wedge -\Delta q_t \neq \emptyset) \end{aligned} \qquad (4.10)$$

$$P(\omega_t = \text{Exploitation}|\Delta q_t, D_{t-1}) = \begin{aligned} & P(+\Delta q_t \neq \emptyset \wedge +\Delta q_t \in D_{t-1}) \\ & + P(+\Delta q_t = \emptyset \wedge -\Delta q_t = \emptyset) \end{aligned} \qquad (4.11)$$

where D_{t-1} include all clicked documents and all snippets that are ranked higher than the last clicked document at iteration $t-1$. User actions a_u include the current query changes $+\Delta q_t$ and $-\Delta q_t$. In fact, $P(\omega_t|\Delta q_t, D_{t-1})$ needs to be calculated for each specific case.

For instance,

$$P(\omega_t = \text{Exploration}|a = \text{"delete term"}, \Delta q_t, D_{t-1}) = \frac{\text{\# of observed true explorations due to deleting terms}}{\text{\# of observed explorations due to deleting terms}}. \qquad (4.12)$$

Here only the actions with "deleted terms" are illustrated. "# of observed explorations" is the number of observed explorations suggesting that the user is likely to explore another subtopic based on Eq. 4.10, while "# of observed true explorations" is the number of observed explorations judged positive by human accessors in a ground truth. The annotations can be found online.[3]

4.3.3 BELIEF UPDATES

At every search iteration the belief state b is updated twice; once at Step 3, another at Step 8. It reflects the interaction and cooperative game between the two agents.

A belief $b_t(s_i)$ is defined as $P(s_i|a_t, b_t)$. The initial belief states can be calculated as: $b_0(s_i = S_z) = P(s_i = S_x)P(s_i = S_y)$, where $x \in \{R = Rel, NR = Non\text{-}Rel\}$, $y \in \{R = exploRation, T = exploiTation\}$, z is the cross-product of x and y and $z \in \{RR, RT, NRR, NRT\}$. In addition, $0 \leq b(s_i) \leq 1$ and $\sum_{s_i} b(s_i) = 1$.

The belief update function is $b_{t+1}(s_j) = P(s_j|\omega_t, a_t, b_t)$ by taking into account new observations ω_t. It is updated from iteration t to iteration $t+1$:

$$b_{t+1}(s_j) \stackrel{def}{=\!=} P(s_j|\omega_t, a_t, b_t)$$
$$= \frac{O(s_j, a_t, \omega_t) \sum_{s_i \in S} T(s_i, a_t, s_j) b_t(s_i)}{P(\omega_t|a_t, b_t)} \qquad (4.13)$$

where s_i and s_j are two states, $i, j \in \{RR, RT, NRR, NRT\}$. t indices the search iterations, and $O(s_j, a_t, \omega_t) = P(\omega_t|s_j, a_t)$ is calculated based on Section 4.3.2. $P(\omega_t|a_t, b_t)$ is the normalization factor to keep $\sum_{s_i \in S} b(s_i) = 1$. For notation simplicity, we will only use a to represent actions from now on. However, it is worth noting that actions can be both domain-level actions a and messages Σ.

---

[3]The manual annotations for "exploration" transitions can be found at `www.cs.georgetown.edu/~huiyang/win-win`.

Transition probability $T(s_i, a_t, s_j)$ is defined as $P(s_j | s_i, a_t, b_t)$. It describes the transition probability from one state to another state based on taking action a_t, $s_i \rightarrow s_j$, and can be estimated by Maximum Likelihood Estimation (MLE). It can be calculated as $T(s_i, a_t, s_j) = \frac{\#Transition(s_i, a_t, s_j)}{\#Transition(s_i, a_t, s*)}$, where Transition (s_i, a_t, s_j) is the sum of all transitions that start at state s_i, take action a_t and land at state s_j. Transition $(s_i, a_t, s*)$ is the sum of all transitions that start at state s_i and land at any state by action a_t.

Finally, taking $O(s_j, a_t, \omega_t) = P(\omega_t | s_j, a_t)$, which also equals to $P(\omega_t | s_j, a_t, b_t)$ when considering beliefs, and $T(s_i, a_t, s_j) = P(s_j | s_i, a_t, b_t)$, the updated belief can be written as:

$$
\begin{aligned}
b_{t+1}(s_j) &= \frac{P(\omega_t | s_j, a_t, b_t) \sum_{s_i \in S} P(s_j | s_i, a_t, b_t) b_t(s_i)}{P(\omega_t | a_t, b_t)} \\
&= \frac{P(\omega_t | s_j, a_t, b_t) \sum_{s_i \in S} P(s_j | s_i, a_t, b_t) b_t(s_i)}{\sum_{s_k \in S} P(\omega_t | s_k, a_t) \sum_{s_i \in S} P(s_k | s_i, a_t) b_t(s_i)}
\end{aligned}
\tag{4.14}
$$

where $b_t(s_i)$ is $P(s_i | a_t, b_t)$, whose initial value is $b_0(s_i)$.

4.4 RETRIEVAL FOR SESSIONS

A general observation in session search is that the influence of previous queries and previous search results to the most recent query diminishes over search iterations. A user's desire for novel documents also supports this argument. As such, in the query change model, reinforcement learning is applied backward, that is, instead of discounting future rewards, past rewards are discounted instead. The result is that recent queries and search results are given a higher priority than those that occurred further in the past.

In session search, the objective is to retrieve relevant documents for query q_t, which is equivalent to finding a ranking of documents that maximizes the reward function. That is to say, the task of retrieval documents for a session is equivalent to finding the best policy in a Dynamic IR system. Inspired by the Bellman equation, the relevance of a document d can be modeled as:

$$
\mathcal{R}(q_t, d) = P(q_t | d) + \gamma \sum_a P(q_t | q_{t-1}, D_{t-1}, a) \max_{D_{t-1}} P(q_{t-1} | D_{t-1})
\tag{4.15}
$$

which recursively calculates the reward starting from q_1 and continues with the search engine agent's policy until the query at iteration t. $\gamma \in (0, 1)$ is the discount factor, $\max_{D_{t-1}} P(q_{t-1} | D_{t-1})$ is the maximum of the past rewards, $P(q_t | d)$ is the current reward, and $P(q_t | q_{t-1}, D_{t-1}, a)$ is the query transition model.

It is worthy noting that Dynamic IR models for session search is still a retrieval model, which adapts the spirit of reinforcement learning but does not directly use the learning framework for retrieval. For instance, the policies that a search engine should follow to select the best actions to return a good set of documents can be obtained by a set of heuristics developed by IR researchers [95]. The policies can also be learned via adapted Q-functions to take into account the joint optimization from both the user side and the search engine side [169]. We describe the current retrieval methods in this section.

Table 4.4: Search engine agent's policy. Actions are adjustments on the term weights. ↑ means increasing, ↓ means decreasing and → means keeping the original term weight.

	$\epsilon\ D_{t-1}$	Action	Example from TREC Session Track
q_{theme}	Y	↑	"pocono mountain" in s6
	N	↑	"france world cup 98 reaction" in s28, $q_1 \rightarrow q_2$
$+\Delta q$	Y	↓	"policy" in s37, $q_1 \rightarrow q_2$
	N	↑	"U.S." in s37, $q_1 \rightarrow q_2$
$-\Delta q$	Y	↓	"reaction" in s28, $q_2 \rightarrow q_3$
	N	→	"legislation" in s32, $q_2 \rightarrow q_3$

4.4.1   OBTAINING THE POLICIES BY HEURISTICS

In Dynamic IR models, a search engine agent performs actions based on the user agent's actions. The user's actions must be identified in order to do this. For instance, query change Δq must be observed before the search engine takes actions. The query change Δq can be recognized by string matching. First, q_{theme} is generated based on the *Longest Common Subsequence (LCS)* [106] in both q_{t-1} and q_t. A subsequence is a sequence that appears in two strings in the same relative order but is not necessarily continuous. The LCS can be the common prefix or the common suffix of the two queries; it can also consist of several discontinuous common parts from the two queries. Take session 6 $q_6 \rightarrow q_7$ as an example: q_6="pocono mountains camelbeach hotel," q_7="pocono mountains chateau resort," q_{theme} = LCS(q_6, q_7) = "pocono mountains." Next, added terms $+\Delta q$ are recognized as are removed terms $-\Delta q$. Generally, the terms that occur in the current query but not in the previous query constitute $+\Delta q$; while the terms that occur in the previous query but not in the current query constitute $-\Delta q$. In the above example, $-\Delta q_7$ = "camelbeach hotel," and $+\Delta q_7$ = "chateau resort."

Table 4.4 summarizes a search engine policy chosen heuristically from observations made on query changes occurring in search logs. The search engine agent observes query change from the user agent and takes corresponding actions. For each type of query change, *theme terms*, *added terms* and *removed terms*, term weights can be adjusted accordingly for better retrieval accuracy. The search engine agent's potential actions include *increasing*, *decreasing* and *maintaining* the term weights. Based on the observed query change as well as whether the query terms appeared in the previous search results D_{t-1}, we can sense whether the user will favor the query terms in the current run of search. Table 4.4 illustrates the policies for the search engine agent.

Theme terms q_{theme} often appear in many queries in a session and there is a strong preference for them. Thus, they are used to increase the weights of theme terms whether they appeared in D_{t-1} or not (rows 1 and 2 in the table). In the latter case, if a theme term was not found in D_{t-1} (the top retrieval results), it is likely that the documents containing them were ranked low. Therefore, the weights of theme terms need to be raised to boost the rankings of those documents (row 2 in the table). However, since theme terms are topic words in a session, they could appear like stopwords within the session. To avoid biasing the model too much toward them, their term weights are lowered proportionally to their numbers of occurrences in D_{t-1}.

For added terms $+\Delta q$, if they occurred in previous search results D_{t-1}, their term weights are decreased for the sake of novelty [118]. For example, in session 5 $q_1 \rightarrow q_2$, "pocono mountains"→"pocono mountains park," the added term "park" appeared in a document in D_5. If the original weight of "park" was used, this document might still be ranked high in D_2 and the user may dislike it since he read it before. Hence, the added terms' weights are decreased if they are in D_{t-1} (row 3 in Table 4.4). On the other hand, if the added terms did not occur in D_{t-1}, they are the new search focus and so their term weigh "policy," occurred in D_1 whereas the other part, "US," did not. To respect the user's preference, the weight of "US" is increased while decreasing that of "policy" to penalize documents about other "polices" including "Canada policy."

For removed terms $-\Delta q$, if they appeared in D_{t-1}, their term weights are decreased since the user dislikes them by deleting them (row 5 in the table). For example, in session 28 $q_2 \rightarrow q_3$, "reaction" existed in D_2 and is removed in q_3. However, if the removed terms are not in D_{t-1}, their weights are not changed since they are already removed from q_t by the user (row 6 in the table).

By considering all possible cases in the policy, the transition model as part of Eq. (4.15) can be expanded for each case. Therefore, the relevance score between the current query q_t and a document d can be written as

$$
\begin{aligned}
Score(q_t, d) = \log P(q_t|d) + \alpha \sum_{w \in q_{theme}} \left[1 - P\left(w|d_{t-1}^*\right)\right] \log P\left(w|d\right) \\
- \beta \sum_{\substack{t \in +\Delta q \\ w \in d_{t-1}^*}} P\left(w|d_{t-1}^*\right) \log P\left(w|d\right) \\
+ \epsilon \sum_{\substack{w \in +\Delta q \\ w \notin d_{t-1}^*}} idf(w) \log P(w|d) \\
- \delta \sum_{w \in -\Delta q} P\left(w|d_{t-1}^*\right) \log P\left(w|d\right) \quad (4.16)
\end{aligned}
$$

where $P(q_t|d)$ can be a relevance score returned by any adhoc retrieval algorithms. α, β, ϵ and δ are term re-weighting weights for each types of actions. Note that different parameters β and δ are applied on $+\Delta q$ and $-\Delta q$, since added terms and removed terms may affect the retrieval differently. The best term re-weighting parameters reported in [95] for theme terms are $\alpha = 2.2$, for added old terms $\beta = 1.8$, for added new terms $\epsilon = 0.07$ and for removed terms $\theta = 0.4$.

To obtain a maximum reward from all possible reward functions $P(q_{t-1}|d_{t-1})$, i.e., the text relevance of previous query q_{t-1} and all previous search results $d_{t-1} \in D_{t-1}$, a *maximum rewarding document* can be generated, denoted as d_{t-1}^*. Further to this, the candidates for the

d_{t-1}^* should only be selected from the effective previous search results D_{t-1}^e. The document d_{t-1}^* is defined as the documents that are the most relevant to q_{t-1}.

The overall document relevance score $Score_{session}(q_n, d)$ for a session that starts at q_1 and ends at q_n by considering all queries in the session:

$$Score_{session}(q_n, d) = Score(q_n, d) + \gamma Score_{session}(q_{n-1}, d) \tag{4.17}$$

$$= Score(q_n, d) + \gamma \left[Score(q_{n-1}, d) + \gamma Score_{session}(q_{n-2}, d) \right] \tag{4.18}$$

$$= \sum_{t=1}^{n} \gamma^{n-i} Score(q_t, d) \tag{4.19}$$

where $q_1, q_2, \ldots, q_n$ are in the same session, and $\gamma \in (0, 1)$ is the discount factor. Eq. (4.19) provides a form of aggregation over the relevance functions of all the queries in a session.

4.4.2 OBTAINING THE POLICIES BY JOINT OPTIMIZATION

After every search iteration, the best policy should be determined for picking up the best actions for the search engine agent. For all $a \in A_{se}$, we write the search engine's Q-function, which represents the search engine agent's long-term reward, as:

$$Q_{se}(b, a) = \rho(b, a) + \gamma \sum_{\omega \in \Omega} P(\omega|b, a_u, \Sigma_{se}) P(\omega|b, \Sigma_u) \max_a Q_{se}(b', a) \tag{4.20}$$

where the reward for a belief state b is $\rho(b, a) = \sum_{s \in S} b(s) R(s, a)$. $P(\omega|b, a_u, \Sigma_{se})$ corresponds to Eq. 4.10 and Eq. 4.11, and $P(\omega|b, \Sigma_u)$ corresponds to Eq. 4.5 and Eq. 4.6. b' is the updated belief state.

In Dynamic IR models, both the search engine reward and the user reward are taken into account. As in [95], Q_u is calculated as the long-term reward for the user agent:

$$\begin{aligned} Q_u(b, a_u) &= R(s, a_u) + \gamma \sum_{a_u} T(s_t|s_{t-1}, D_{t-1}) \max_{s_{t-1}} Q_u(s_{t-1}, a_u) \\ &= P(q_t|d) + \gamma \sum_a P(q_t|q_{t-1}, D_{t-1}, a) \max_{D_{t-1}} P(q_{t-1}|D_{t-1}) \end{aligned} \tag{4.21}$$

which recursively calculates the reward starting from q_1 and continues with the policy until q_t. $P(q_t|d)$ is the current reward that the user gains through reading the documents. $\max_{D_{t-1}} P(q_{t-1}|D_{t-1})$ is the maximum of the past rewards. The formula matches well with common search scenarios where the user makes decisions about their next actions based on the most relevant document(s) they examined in the previous run of retrieval. Such a document is called *maximum rewarding document(s)*. The document with the largest $P(q_{t-1}|d_{t-1})$ is used as the maximum rewarding document. $P(q_{t-1}|d_{t-1})$ is calculated as $1 - \prod_{t \in q_{t-1}} \{1 - P(t|d_{t-1})\}$, where $P(t|d_{t-1}) = \frac{\#(t, d_{t-1})}{|d_{t-1}|}$, $\#(t, d_{t-1})$ is the number of occurrences of term t in document d_{t-1}, and $|d_{t-1}|$ is the document length.

By optimizing both long-term rewards for the user and for the search engine, the best policy π is used to predict the next action for the search engine. The joint optimization for the dual-agent stochastic game can be represented as:

$$a_{se} = \arg\max_a \left(Q_{se}(b, a) + Q_u(b, a_u) \right) \tag{4.22}$$

where $a_{se} \in A_{se}$ at $t = n$ and n is the number of search iterations in a session, i.e., the session length.

In Dynamic IR models, A_{se} can include many search engine actions. One type of actions is adjusting a query's term weight, assuming the query is reformulated from the previous query by adding $+\Delta q$ or deleting $-\Delta q$. That is to say, $A_{se} = \{$increasing, decreasing, or keeping term weights$\}$. The term weights are increased or decreased by multiplying a factor. A range of search techniques/algorithms can be used as action options for the search engine agent.

4.5   RELATED WORK

Related to dynamic search is the area of task-based search which is an important and emerging field in IR. The dynamics of tasks poses many challenges for the next generation of search engines, for instance, Raman et al. [191] studied a particular case in task-based search where the search topics contain intrinsically diversified tasks. Moreover, the recent National Science Foundation task-based search workshop [137] blueprints provide a roadmap of research in the field, with a focus on incorporating models of tasks, task-types and user information needs into systems to support session search. The work by Scholer et al. [214] examined the effect of threshold priming on users' calibration of relevance. They observed that users' relevance judgments are dynamic: users who are exposed to only non-relevant documents early on tend to assign higher relevance scores compared with users who are exposed to both low and highly relevant documents early on. Sakai and Dou [206] presented a comprehensive whole-session evaluation framework for evaluating summaries, ranked document lists and multi-query sessions from the text actually examined by a user during a session. Finally, Radlinski and Craswell [188] used reinforcement learning techniques to dynamically evaluate interleaved rankings over time.

Session search has attracted a great amount of research from a variety of views [45, 95, 145, 191, 276]. There is a large body of work using query logs to study queries and sessions. Feild and Allan [80] proposed a task-aware model for query recommendation using a random walk over a term-query graph from query logs. Song and He [232] worked on optimal rare query suggestion also using random walk and implicit feedback in logs. Wang et al. [248] utilized a semi-supervised clustering model based on a latent structural SVM to extract cross-dynamic search tasks. Many recent log-based approaches also appear in the Web Search Click Data (WCSD) workshop series.[4] These works could be grouped as log-based methods.

Another large group of works are content-based methods, which directly study the content of the query and the document. For instance, Raman et al. [191] studied a particular case in dynamic search where the search topics contain intrinsically diversified tasks, which typically require

---

[4]http://research.microsoft.com/en-us/um/people/nickcr/wscd2014/

multi-dynamic searches on different aspects of an information need. They applied techniques used in diversity web search to dynamic search. Content-based dynamic search also includes most research generated from the recent TREC Session Tracks. Guan et al. [93] organized phrase structure in queries within a session to improve retrieval effectiveness. Jiang et al. [118] proposed an adaptive browsing model that handles novelty in dynamic search. Jiang and He [116] further analyzed the effects of past queries and click-through information on whole-dynamic search effectiveness.

An advanced area of study has been investigating search across multiple sessions [162]. Kotov et al. [145] proposed methods for modeling and analyzing users' search behaviors that extend over multiple search sessions. Wang et al. [248] targeted the identification of cross-session (long-term) search tasks by investigating inter-query dependencies learned from user behaviors; they focused on the long-term user history with multiple search sessions.

Prior to these recent MDP and POMDP approaches, earlier work has presented similar ideas. Shen et al. [219] proposed a user model to infer a user's interest from the search context, such as previous queries and click data in a same search session, for the task of personalized search. The focus of this task is the user, instead of a single query or a series of queries. A user model is maintained for a specific user and all the documents are re-ranked immediately after the model is updated. Under a decision-theoretic framework, they treated Web search as a decision process with *user actions*, *search engine responses to actions* and *user models* based on the Bayesian decision theory. In order to choose an optimal system response, it introduces a *loss function* defined on the space of responses and user models. The loss function depends on the responses thus is inevitably application-dependent. This model can detect search session boundaries automatically. However, there are no states and no transitions defined in this model.

Jin et al. [120] provided another POMDP model for document re-ranking over multiple result pages in order to improve the online diversity of search results by considering implicit user feedback in the exploration search phase. Similar to dynamic search, the task is a kind of interactive search for a single intent. The main difference of this task from dynamic search is that it aims at a sequence of search pages for a single query, rather than a series of queries. The hidden states in this model were the probability distribution of document relevance, and the beliefs were derived by a multivariate Gaussian distribution. This approach assumed that the document relevancy to a single query could not be affected by the interactions between the user and the search engine in the multi-page document re-ranking and be invariant in different search pages. Therefore, there was no state transition in its model. This is one major difference between [120] and other typical POMDP models, including [169]. The search engine actions that they used were ranked lists of documents, which were termed as *portfolios*. The nDCG metric was regarded as a measure of reward in this approach.

Similarly, Zhang et al. [277] used portfolios as actions when re-ranking documents in dynamic search by using a POMDP. In order to decrease the numerous possible actions, they grouped these actions into four high-level action strategies. For the same purpose, a fixed small number of two hidden states were defined to indicate document relevance. Such a state definition could be viewed as a subset of states [169]. Zhang et al.'s approach considered both global rewards and local rewards. The former was a measure to the relevance of a document based on multiple users and multiple sessions, and could be estimated from the sessions recorded in the query log. The latter was a measure to document relevance based on the current session. It was calculated by the Q-learning method.

CHAPTER 5

Dynamic IR for Recommender Systems

In this chapter we explore the areas of collaborative filtering and recommendation in the context of DIR. We learned in Chapter 4 that for session search, in order to fulfill an information need, the dynamic process involved a single user interacting with a search system in a complex way over a series of steps. In this chapter, we give a further example and its formulation on how a user interacts with a recommender system over a period of time.

We start by giving an overview of static collaborative filtering and recommendation and their mainstream mathematical models. This is then extended to a dynamic case and it is explained how they fit into the DIR model. We describe a number of useful and important multi-armed bandit algorithms that have been used in recommendation as well as other similar contexts.

5.1 COLLABORATIVE FILTERING

Collaborative filtering (CF) is concerned with predicting the probability that a specific user will like certain information items (books, movies, music items, web pages, etc). As the term "collaborative" implies, the prediction relies on collaborative intelligence from a collection of other (similar) users' preferences, which have been previously collected. Originally, the idea of collaborative filtering was derived from heuristics. Goldberg et al [92] coined the term "collaborative filtering" while developing an automatic filtering system for electronic mail, called *Tapestry*, at Xerox Palo Alto Research:

> *"Collaborative filtering simply means that people collaborate to help one another perform filtering by recording their reactions to documents they read. Such reactions may be that a document was particularly interesting (or particularly uninteresting)..."*

One of the popular applications of collaborative filtering is personalized recommendation. For instance, in movie recommendation, a user is first asked explicitly to rate what he or she has liked or disliked in the past. Then, after providing ratings for a few movie items that they know, the recommendation engine would be able to produce a prediction about the user's ratings of unseen movie items, by looking at other similar users' past ratings for the movie items in question. In this case, users have to explicitly provide their ratings for movies items beforehand, e.g., give 1 star for the lowest rating and 5 stars for the highest rating.

However, end users sometimes find it is time-consuming to provide such explicit ratings. Alternatively, it is possible for a recommendation system to unobtrusively observe the users' actions and choices and infer their preferences from historic interactions. For example, Amazon's[1] book recommendation makes use of the users' purchase records and browsing behavior to make recommendations in the form of "Customers Who Bought This Item Also Bought ..." [161].

In either case, if we look at the recommendation problem at a conceptual level, it is very much like search. This is because, as we have discussed in the previous chapters, the solution still requires calculating the correspondence (called relevance) between a user information need (in our case, a user preference or predefined preferable topics) and an information item (e.g., a movie or a book). In textual retrieval, the correspondence is usually calculated by looking at content descriptions, e.g., how many and how frequent the query terms occur within a document.

By the same token, when we make personalized recommendations, it is possible that users' unseen preference is predicted by examining the match between the textual descriptions of information needs and information items. Such a technique is called content-based filtering [21]. Collaborative filtering, on the other hand, does not necessarily need textual descriptions to make the match. It makes personalized recommendations by aggregating the opinions and preferences from previous users, not limited to *this* user alone. Further to this, given that recommendations tend to be delivered as a stream rather than all at once, similarities exist between this work and that on adaptive filtering described in the previous chapter. Collaborative filtering can be considered the case where user profiles learned using adaptive filtering are applied across a population of users.

5.2   STATIC RECOMMENDATION

In the simple static setting, the recommendation task aims at predicting an unknown rating of an item from the user, given other observed ratings from this user and other users about this item and other items. It is essentially a missing data prediction problem. To illustrate this, consider the example user-item matrix in Table 5.1, where we have observed ratings from four users about 7 movies. Not all of the entries are observed; in fact, in a real dataset, most of the entries would be missing. The task for recommendation is to infer the missing ratings from the observed ones. For instance, we might want to predict user *Bori*'s rating on the movie "Love Actually" based on his previous ratings on the other movies and the other three users' historic ratings in the table.

5.2.1   USER-BASED APPROACHES

The most commonly used approach is the user-based method, which assumes that users who have similar preferences in the past are likely to have similar preferences in the future, and the more similar they are, the more likely they are to agree with each other in the future [103]. From the table, we can see that user *Boris*'s preference is similar to both *Dave* and *Jane*—all of them love

---

[1]http://www.amazon.com

Table 5.1: A sample User-Item matrix. Each entry in the matrix is a rating made by a user to an item (a movie in this case), representing their preference toward the particular item.

	Die Hard	Skyfall	Casino Royale	Titanic	Notting Hill	About Time	Love Actually
Boris	* * *	* * * * *			*		?
Dave		* * * * *	* * * * *				*
Will				* * * * *	* * * * *	* * *	* * * *
Jane	* * * *	* * * *	* * * *				* *

actions movies, implied by their high ratings for "Die Hard," "Skyfall," and/or "Casio Royale." As both *Dave* and *Jane* gave low ratings to movie "Love Actually," we can reasonably infer that *Boris* would have also given a low rating if he had seen the movie. The user-based preference prediction is therefore calculated by weighted averaging of the ratings from similar users

$$\hat{r}_{u,i} = \bar{r}_u + \sum_v w_{v,u}(r_{v,i} - \bar{r}_v), \tag{5.1}$$

where $\hat{r}_{u,i}$ is the predicted rating of user u for item i, where u is user index and i is item index ($u \in \{1, ..., M\}$ and $i \in \{1, ..., N\}$). M denotes the number of users whereas N denotes the number of items. $\bar{r}_u$ and $\bar{r}_u$ denote the average ratings from user u and user v, respectively. $w_{v,u}$ denotes the similarity between user v and user u, acting as the weight. Cosine similarity and Pearson's correlation coefficient are weights commonly used in practice. $r_{v,i}$ is the observed rating of user v about item i. The user-based approach resembles a nearest neighbor method because usually the top-k closest users are chosen instead of averaging across all the users, where k can be determined empirically.

5.2.2   PROBABILISTIC MATRIX FACTORIZATION

A model can also be built using hidden variables. Matrix Factorization is a method of using several (typically two) lower-dimensional matrices to approximate the original matrix in order to re-discover the missing entries [212], i.e.,

$$\hat{r}_{u,i} = p'_u q_i, \tag{5.2}$$

where the prediction is made by a dot product between a user feature hidden vector p_u and an item feature hidden vector q_i. We use a ′ to define the transpose. p_u and q_i have the same dimension, which is much smaller than either M or N. Both of the hidden vectors can be learned by Alternating Least Squares or Stochastic Gradient Descent methods [144].

The **Probabilistic Matrix Factorization (PMF)** model [209] aims to build the distributions for the user and the item hidden feature vectors, which are then used to generate the samples.

Specifically, the conditional probability distribution of the rating given the user and item feature vectors follows a Gaussian distribution

$$P(r_{ui}|\boldsymbol{p}'_u\boldsymbol{q}_i,\sigma^2) = \mathcal{N}(r_{ui}|\boldsymbol{p}'_u\boldsymbol{q}_i,\sigma^2). \tag{5.3}$$

We can thus express the likelihood function of the model parameters (the joint probability of the observed data given the model) as:

$$P(R|P,Q,\sigma^2) = \prod_{u=1}^{M}\prod_{i=1}^{N}[\mathcal{N}(r_{ui}|\boldsymbol{p}'_u\boldsymbol{q}_i,\sigma^2)]^{\delta_{ui}}, \tag{5.4}$$

where $\delta_{ij} = 1$ if user u rated item i and $\delta_{ij} = 0$ otherwise. R is the user-item matrix. P and Q are denoted as the user or item feature vector matrix, where each row vector represents a user or item feature vector $P = [\boldsymbol{p}_1,\boldsymbol{p}_2,\ldots,\boldsymbol{p}_M]'$, $Q = [\boldsymbol{q}_1,\boldsymbol{q}_2,\ldots,\boldsymbol{q}_N]'$.

The prior distributions of the user and item feature vectors can be described as Gaussian again with prior variances σ_p^2 and σ_q^2, e.g.,

$$P(\boldsymbol{p}_u|\sigma_p^2) = \mathcal{N}(\boldsymbol{p}_u|\boldsymbol{0},\sigma_p^2 I), \tag{5.5}$$

$$P(\boldsymbol{q}_i|\sigma_q^2) = \mathcal{N}(\boldsymbol{q}_i|\boldsymbol{0},\sigma_q^2 I). \tag{5.6}$$

The above four equations define the generative process of the PMF model: a prior generates the hidden feature vectors $\boldsymbol{p}_u$ and $\boldsymbol{q}_i$. The dot product between the two generated ones with added noise produces the ratings. With the observed ratings R, one can obtain the posterior distributions for the user and item feature vectors [209]. Let us now focus on the conditional distribution of the user and item feature vectors, given the current item/user feature vectors to implement Markov chain Monte Carlo and Gibbs Sampling (MCMC-Gibbs):

$$P(P|R,Q,\sigma^2,\sigma_p^2,\sigma_q^2) = P(R|P,Q,\sigma^2)P(P|\sigma_p^2,\sigma_q^2) \tag{5.7}$$

$$\propto \prod_{u=1}^{M}\mathcal{N}(\boldsymbol{p}_u|\boldsymbol{0},\sigma_p^2 I)\prod_{i=1}^{N}[\mathcal{N}(r_{ui}|\boldsymbol{p}'_u\boldsymbol{q}_i,\sigma^2)]^{\delta_{ui}} \tag{5.8}$$

$$\propto \prod_{u=1}^{M}\exp\left[-\frac{1}{2\sigma^2}\left(\frac{\sigma^2}{\sigma_p^2}\boldsymbol{p}'_u\boldsymbol{p}_u + \sum_{\delta_{ui}=1}(r_{ui}-\boldsymbol{p}'_u\boldsymbol{q}_i)^2\right)\right] \tag{5.9}$$

$$\propto \prod_{u=1}^{M}\exp\left[-\frac{1}{2\sigma^2}\left(\boldsymbol{p}'_u(\sum_{\delta_{ui}=1}\boldsymbol{q}_i\boldsymbol{q}'_i + \frac{\sigma^2}{\sigma_p^2}I)\boldsymbol{p}_u - 2\sum_{\delta_{ui}=1}r_{ui}\boldsymbol{q}'_i\boldsymbol{p}_u\right)\right] \tag{5.10}$$

$$\propto \prod_{u=1}^{M}\mathcal{N}(\boldsymbol{p}_u|\boldsymbol{\mu}_u,\Sigma_u). \tag{5.11}$$

This means that for each user its feature vector follows a Gaussian distribution given item feature vectors:

$$P(p_u|R, Q, \sigma^2, \sigma_p^2, \sigma_q^2) = \mathcal{N}(p_u|\mu_u, \Sigma_u), \tag{5.12}$$
$$\mu_u = (D_u' D_u + \lambda_p I)^{-1} D_u' r_u, \tag{5.13}$$
$$\Sigma_u = (D_u' D_u + \lambda_p I)^{-1} \sigma^2. \tag{5.14}$$

Here, D_u is the observational matrix for the user, each row of which is the feature vectors of the user-rated items sampled from their posteriors. r_u denotes the vector of corresponding ratings of these items for the given user u, and $\lambda_p = \sigma^2/\sigma_p^2$.

Similarly, the posterior distribution for the item feature vector q_i conditioned on the sampled user feature vectors can be obtained as

$$P(q_i|R, P, \sigma^2, \sigma_p^2, \sigma_q^2) = \mathcal{N}(q_i|\nu_i, \Psi_i), \tag{5.15}$$
$$\nu_i = (B_i' B_i + \lambda_q I)^{-1} B_i' r_i, \tag{5.16}$$
$$\Psi_i = (B_i' B_i + \lambda_q I)^{-1} \sigma^2, \tag{5.17}$$

where B_i is the observational matrix with each row the sampled user feature vector.

The distributions converge as alternatively sampling the item and the user feature vectors according to the conditional distributions for them. Then both the expected user and item feature vectors (μ_u and ν_i) and their uncertainties (Σ_u and Ψ_i) are obtained.

5.3   DYNAMICS IN RECOMMENDATION

Although collaborative filtering exists in various forms in practice, its purposes can be generally regarded as "item ranking" and "rating prediction," as illustrated in Figure 5.1. Both of them require constant dynamical updates. The rating prediction (see Figure 5.1a and b) aims to predict an unknown rating of an item for a target user, with the requirement that the user has to explore first and explicitly rate a certain number of items. Moreover, in many practical systems *Last.fm*,[2] it is sometimes more favorable to formulate collaborative filtering as a dynamic item-ranking problem, because we often face a situation where our ultimate task is to receive user feeback and to constantly generate the top-N list of the end user's most favorite items (see Figure 5.1c and d).

Let us now formulate dynamics in recommendation. Suppose the system has N items and M users. The ratings between them are recorded in the preference matrix $R_{M \times N}$ in which each element $r_{u,i}$ is the observed rating from the user u to the item i. Without loss of generality, we consider the following process in discrete timesteps. Suppose the target user is now denoted simply by u. At each timestep $t \in [1, 2, \ldots, T]$, the system delivers (recommends) an item to the target user. The user will then give feedback in the form of ratings, or "like" and "dislike," or ignore the recommendation ("unknown"). In either way, we denote the feedback as $r_{u,i(t)}$, the rating collected by the system from user u to the recommended item $i(t)$ at timestep t. In other

---

[2]http://last.fm

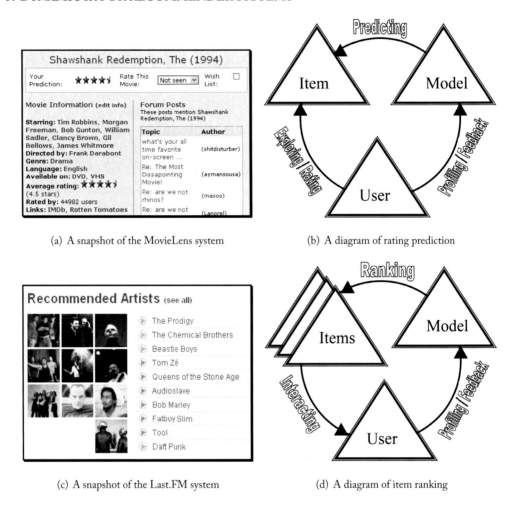

(a) A snapshot of the MovieLens system

(b) A diagram of rating prediction

(c) A snapshot of the Last.FM system

(d) A diagram of item ranking

Figure 5.1: The two forms of dynamic recommendation.

words, $r_{u,i(t)}$ is the "reward" collected by the system from this target user. After receiving the feedback, the system updates its model and decides on which item to recommend next.

5.3.1   OBJECTIVE FUNCTION

Let's denote $\mathcal{H}(t)$ as the available information at t the system has for the target user

$$\mathcal{H}(t) = \{i(1), r_{u,i(1)}, \ldots, i(t-1), r_{u,i(t-1)}\}. \tag{5.18}$$

The item is selected according to a strategy π, which is defined as a function from the current information to the selected item:

$$i(t) \equiv \pi(\mathcal{H}(t)) \, . \tag{5.19}$$

The optimal strategy should maximize the cumulated expected rewards during T timesteps,

$$i^*(\cdot) = \operatorname*{argmax}_{i(\cdot)} \sum_{t=1}^{T} \mathrm{E}[r_{u,i(t)}], \tag{5.20}$$

where $i(\cdot) = \{i(1), i(2), \ldots, i(T)\}$ and $i(t)$ means the item selected at timestep t. Here we consider the quality of recommendations at different timesteps as equally important, and summarize the user's overall satisfaction at a given period T.

This objective falls into the target of the multi-armed bandit problem, where we regard each item as each arm of the bandit. The next questions are how to estimate the reward and how to optimize the objective function. Using a factor model explained above [109, 209], the rating is a product of user and item feature vectors p_u and q_i. This is widely used in many CF algorithms:

$$r_{u,i} = p'_u q_i + \eta, \tag{5.21}$$

where $\eta \sim \mathcal{N}(0, \sigma^2)$ is the observation noise. The objective function is then re-formulated as follows:

$$i^*(\cdot) = \operatorname*{argmax}_{i(\cdot)} \sum_{t=1}^{T} \mathrm{E}_{p_u, q_i(t)}[p'_u q_{i(t)} | t]. \tag{5.22}$$

The question now is how to optimize the objective function.

5.3.2   USER DYNAMICS

Both the p_u and $q_{i(t)}$ are random variables following certain distributions. A heuristic solution is to choose an item according to its probability of being optimal [52].

$$p(i(t) = i) = \int \mathbb{I}\left[\mathrm{E}(r_{ui} | p_u, q_i) = \max_i \mathrm{E}(r_{ui} | p_u, q_i)\right] \cdot$$
$$p(p_u, q_i | t) d q_i d p_u, \tag{5.23}$$

where $\mathbb{I}$ is the indicator function. The integration is usually intractable or computationally expensive [52]. Therefore, the Thompson sampling algorithm is leveraged to approach the integration in Eq. (5.23). By Thompson sampling, the integration is circumvented by sampling the user and item feature vectors from their distributions, and picking the item that leads to the largest expectation of the reward:

$$i^*(t)_{ts} = \operatorname*{argmax}_i \mathrm{E}(r_{ui} | \tilde{p}_u, \tilde{q}_i), \tag{5.24}$$

where $\tilde{p}_u$ and $\tilde{q}_i$ mean the sampled user and item feature vectors. Thompson sampling has been proven to be effective and it is flexible with respect to the forms of the reward function [52].

Thompson Sampling

Thompson sampling can be implemented according to the distributions and they can be updated online whenever new ratings are collected by the system. However, in the dynamic collaborative filtering scenario, the distribution of the target user's feature vector is much more sensitive to his/her feedback on the items. On the item side, since each item has usually collected relatively sufficient ratings, it is not necessary to retrain its feature vector immediately after receiving each rating from the target user, and we choose to periodically retrain them. Therefore, we simply use the notation $\tilde{q}_i$ to express sampled item feature vector from the presently calculated item feature vector distribution. For the target user, its observational matrix grows each time, and its distribution can be described similarly conditioned on the observations:

$$\tilde{p}_{u,t} \sim \mathcal{N}(p_{u,t}|\mu_{u,t}, \Sigma_{u,t}), \tag{5.25}$$

where

$$\mu_{u,t} = (D'_{u,t} D_{u,t} + \lambda_p I)^{-1} D'_{u,t} r_{u,t}, \tag{5.26}$$
$$\Sigma_{u,t} = (D'_{u,t} D_{u,t} + \lambda_p I)^{-1} \sigma^2. \tag{5.27}$$

Similarly, $D_{u,t}$ is the observational matrix with each row the recommended item feature vector, and $\Sigma_{u,t}$ is the uncertainty of the user feature vector at time t.

From Eq. (5.24), the Thompson sampling method with the PMF modeling suggests to choose the item with the highest value of the inner product of the sampled values, and Eq. (5.24) can be approximated as:

$$i^*(t)_{ts} = \operatorname*{argmax}_{i} \tilde{p}'_{u,t} \tilde{q}_i, \tag{5.28}$$

where $\tilde{p}_{u,t}$ is sampled from the estimated distribution in Eq. (5.25).

Thompson sampling enables exploration through the "width" of the distributions of the inner product of the user and item feature vectors. The "width" further comes from both the uncertainties of the user and item feature vectors. By the Thompson sampling based approach described above, the uncertainties of the user and item feature vectors are considered on the same footing. However, when considering dynamic collaborative filtering as a user-centric scenario, the obtained knowledge on the target user side may be much more important than that on the item side, especially when items have collected many ratings and thus are always already well-learned. Therefore, in the following part, we adopt a biased view so that the item feature vectors are assumed to be well-learned as the maximum a posterior (MAP) solution ν_i from the distributions obtained by PMF, and only the user feature vector distributions are maintained for the sampling process.

5.3.3   ITEM SELECTION VIA CONFIDENCE BOUND

With the item feature vectors known and fixed, the reward in Eq. (5.21) tends to be a linear form with the item feature vectors as coefficients, and the essence of exploration/exploitation is to approach the user feature vector. Therefore, such a problem falls into the framework of the index-based multi-armed bandit algorithms introduced in the previous chapter [9]. In this way, we take the MAP estimation of the item feature vectors ν_i as the representatives of the items and assume them to be fixed.

In the following parts, linear UCB and generalized linear UCB algorithms are presented for our problem respectively. A variation of ϵ-greedy algorithm is also provided for comparison.

Linear UCB

As mentioned above, assuming the item feature vectors as fixed, the reward function reduces to be linear in the item feature vectors, and the objective function in Eq. (5.21) is further written as

$$i^*(\cdot) = \underset{i(\cdot)}{\operatorname{argmax}} \sum_{t=1}^{T} \mathbb{E}[r_{u,i(t)}] \tag{5.29}$$

$$= \underset{i(\cdot)}{\operatorname{argmax}} \sum_{t=1}^{T} \mathbb{E}_{p_u}[p'_u|t]\nu_{i(t)}, \tag{5.30}$$

where $\mathbb{E}_{p_u}[p'_u|t]$ can be estimated according to Eq. (5.26).

The expected user feature vector can be obtained according to Eq. (5.26). Now the uncertainty of the reward can be obtained as the estimated variance of the inner product of the user and item feature vectors $p'_u\nu_i$, which comes from the uncertainty of the estimation in the user feature vector. The estimated variance is the 2-norm based on $\Sigma_{u,t}$ (according to Eq. (5.27), but note that here the observational matrix is made up of the posterior feature vectors of the items):

$$||\nu_i||_{2,\Sigma_{u,t}} \equiv \sqrt{\nu'_i \Sigma_{u,t} \nu_i}. \tag{5.31}$$

According to [247], with the item feature vectors known and fixed, the expectation of the reward by choosing item i is bounded in the interval $\Theta_{i,t}$ with probability at least $1 - \zeta$

$$\Theta_{i,t} = \left[\mu'_{u,t}\nu_i - \alpha||\nu_i||_{2,\Sigma_{u,t}}, \mu'_{u,t}\nu_i + \alpha||\nu_i||_{2,\Sigma_{u,t}}\right] \tag{5.32}$$

where $\alpha = 1 + \sqrt{\ln(2/\zeta)/2}$. The bounded interval motivates a UCB bandit algorithm, i.e., at each timestep, choose the item with the highest upper confidence bound:

$$i^*(t)_l = \underset{i}{\operatorname{argmax}} \left(\mu'_{u,t}\nu_i + \alpha||\nu_i||_{2,\Sigma_{u,t}}\right). \tag{5.33}$$

The algorithm is proven to have a very tight regret bound of $\tilde{O}(\sqrt{T})$ [157], where the regret of an algorithm is defined by the cumulative reward difference to the optimal one.

As defined in Eq. (5.27), matrix $\Sigma_{u,t}$ is a regularized fisher information matrix, measuring how much "information" is known about the user feature vector from the previously recommended items, given the item feature vectors are known already. That is, to recommend an item that maximizes $||\nu_i||_{2,\Sigma_{u,t}}$ is to recommend an item that has been the least represented (understood) by the previously recommended items.

Generalized Linear UCB

The problem can be also linked to the generalized linear bandit problem in [83], which gives a general solution Generalized Linear Model Bandit-Upper Confidence Bound (GLM-UCB) if we assume the reward takes the following form

$$r_{u,i(t)} = \rho\left(p_u' q_{i(t)}\right) + \eta(t), \tag{5.34}$$

where ρ is a monotonically increasing function which can take a linear or nonlinear form. Here we give two options of function ρ, a linear form suggested in Eq. (5.21), and a sigmoid form

$$\rho(p_u' q_i) = \frac{1}{1 + e^{-p_u' q_i}}. \tag{5.35}$$

Similar to the derivations in LinUCB, here the item feature vectors q_i are approximated by the maximum a posterior (MAP) solution ν_i. On the other hand, we need to estimate the user feature vector according to the generalized linear model, which here we denote as $\hat{p}_{u,t}$ (note that here the solution $\hat{p}_{u,t}$ is no longer the MAP solution in Eq. (5.26) due to the nonlinear function ρ). In general, according to [83], the quasi-likelihood estimator $\hat{p}_{u,t}$ of Eq. (5.34) is the solution of

$$\sum_{\tau=1}^{t-1} \left(r_{u,i(\tau)} - \rho(\hat{p}_{u,t}' \nu_{i(\tau)})\right) \nu_{i(\tau)} = 0. \tag{5.36}$$

Specifically, for a sigmoid form, it is estimated as

$$\sum_{\tau=1}^{t-1} \left(r_{u,i(\tau)} - \frac{1}{1 + e^{-\hat{p}_{u,t}' \nu_{i(\tau)}}}\right) \nu_{i(\tau)} = 0. \tag{5.37}$$

For a linear form, the estimate is the same as the maximum posterior estimation of the user feature vectors Eq. (5.26).

The GLM-UCB algorithm follows a similar process as Linear UCB, i.e., firstly $\hat{p}_{u,t}$ is estimated, and the choice of the item is based on the estimated $\hat{p}_{u,t}$ but with exploration part added which is 2-norm based on $\Sigma_{u,t}$ (Eq. (5.31)) multiplied by a factor $c\sqrt{\log t}$ [83]

$$i^*(t)_{gl} = \underset{i}{\operatorname{argmax}} \left(\rho(\hat{p}_{u,t}' \nu_i) + c\sqrt{\log t} \|\nu_i\|_{2,\Sigma_{u,t}}\right). \tag{5.38}$$

Note that the exploration term α is time-dependent:

$$\alpha = \alpha(t) = c\sqrt{\log t}, \tag{5.39}$$

where c is a constant with respect to t [83]. With term $c\sqrt{\log t}$, the decreasing trend of $\|\nu_i\|_{2,\Sigma_{u,t}}$ is weakened so that the exploration level is maintained to some extent. Using the conclusion from [83], GLM-UCB has a regret bound of $\tilde{O}(\sqrt{T})$.[3]

---

[3]The detailed form of the bound is looser than that of LinUCB but it is more general.

Just like the other index-based exploration/exploitation algorithms [9], the algorithms have a low computational complexity, which is $O(T^3 + K^2N)$.

Linear ϵ-greedy

The linear ϵ-greedy algorithm is based on the greedy strategy under our setting, which can be described as

$$i^*(t)_g = \underset{i}{\mathrm{argmax}}\, \mu'_{u,t}\nu_i. \tag{5.40}$$

Because $\mu_{u,t}$ and ν_i can be seen as the MAP solutions for the PMF model, which can also be referred to as the solutions by singular vector decomposition (SVD). We refer to the greedy strategy as greedy SVD, or simply SVD.

The greedy strategy is the myopic strategy that always picks the item leading to the highest expected reward based on current knowledge. ϵ-greedy we adopt here is the naive algorithm which chooses the greedy strategy with probability $1 - \epsilon$ and explores into random items with probability ϵ.

For the above algorithms, two factors contribute to the selection of the item: the exploitation factor suggested by the greedy algorithm Eq. (5.40), and the exploration factor which is controlled by parameters ϵ, α and c, respectively. For each of the three algorithms, the larger the parameter is, the more emphasis is put onto the exploration effort accordingly.

5.4   RELATED WORK

The collaborative filtering research has been traditionally focused on predicting the unknown ratings of a target user as accurately as possible from a collection of user profiles. Major solutions are categorized into two classes: The memory-based methods make the recommendation by explicitly modeling the user or item similarities [73, 103] or combining them together [249], while the model-based methods provide recommendations by developing a "model" of user ratings. For instance, latent factor models have become quite popular during recent years [109], while the matrix factorization techniques [144] have shown their effectiveness in various settings such as the Netflix and Yahoo! music competitions.

A key challenge in CF is to effectively predict preferences for new users, a problem generally referred to as the user cold-start problem [6, 213]. A straightforward method to tackle the problem is to interview the user to provide additional information (e.g., favorite genres) or ask the user to rate a set of items in order to provide enough data for the recommender system. This is a form of relevance feedback that we have explained in the information retrieval case previously. The items used in the interview can be selected based on measures such as popularity, entropy and coverage [193, 194], or a decision tree to partition the users [91, 281]. Active learning is also deployed in order to identify the most informative set of training examples (items) with respect to some selection criterion, such as the expected information gain [99, 119], with the target of minimizing the number of interactions. In sum, all those methods first explicitly figure out the user profile and then use the established user profile to make further recommendations. However, asking users to take interviews is still time-consuming and sometimes a hurdle for a user to overcome even if the effort has been kept to a minimum. By contrast, dynamic collaborative filtering does not distinguish between the stages of learning user profiles and making satisfactory recommendations, but naturally integrates them together. As such, any user, whether a new user or not, can immediately receive sequential recommendations and explore items without overcoming the hassle of providing ratings beforehand.

In the machine learning and statistics communities, the exploration/exploitation problem has been well studied by considering the multi-armed bandit settings [9, 67, 150]. Under the assumption that rewards of arms are independent of each other, ϵ-greedy is a straightforward algorithm that adds a probability of random exploration [10] into a greedy algorithm. The epoch-greedy method generalizes it for the case that the total time T is unknown so that the exploitation and exploration takes place alternatively in each epoch to minimize the regret [150], and it achieves a regret of $\widetilde{O}(T^{2/3})$ with a high probability. The confidence bound algorithms seek to find a region that bounds the expected payoff with a high probability, and within the region, the arm with highest upper confidence bound is selected: the EXP4 approach [15] achieves an $\widetilde{O}(\sqrt{T})$ regret with high probability. A drawback of those approaches lies in that when the number of arms is huge, it becomes difficult to explore. As such, the underlying structure of the arms should be considered. A well-known scenario is that the expected reward is a linear function with respect to the item feature vectors, where the linear bandit algorithm is proposed [9, 71]. On the other hand, in the contextual bandit model with side information, the structure is modeled by positioning each arm into a feature space [78], while a more general linear setting is discussed in [83]. Besides the above algorithms, Thompson sampling yet provides a more flexible way to tackle the multi-armed bandit problems [52] which does not restrict the reward function forms in a linear form.

In the above problems, the item features should be known beforehand, however, when we model the problem with probabilistic matrix factorization (PMF), Thompson sampling [52] provides an empirical solution where the uncertainty of learned feature vectors of both user and item is considered.

The contextual bandit models have been applied to model news article recommendation [157] and online advertising [159], where in each timestep a context (in the form of a feature vector) is revealed, and an arm (either a piece of news or an ad) is selected based on the context. The contextual bandit approaches can be easily applied to both cases because the content features, such as the user's demography and location information, and the item's textual descriptions, can be immediately borrowed to represent the "context." In our domain-free scenario where users or items are presented only by ratings, it is, however, essential to derive a sensible representation for the correlated arms (items) and the context (users).

CHAPTER 6

Evaluating Dynamic IR Systems

IR evaluation is an essential topic in Information Retrieval research. For the dynamic information retrieval models and applications that we present in this book, the complexity in the information seeking process needs to be reflected in evaluation metrics for dynamic models. Dynamic information retrieval often involves information needs that consist of multiple *aspects* or *subtopics*. For example, a lawyer needs to discover various aspects of a lawsuit to find defensive materials. Moreover a complex and task-oriented search process is often time-sensitive. An ideal dynamic search evaluation metric should measure how well a search system allows the user to handle the trade-offs between time taken to search and how well the returned documents cover the different aspects of the information need.

This chapter surveys IR evaluation metrics for Dynamic IR systems, with a focus on a recent evaluation metric—the Cube Test (CT) [166], which was developed based on a novel utility model—the water filling model. The Cube Test measures the speed required to fulfill an overall and multi-faceted information need. It well captures the features and requirements of complex search tasks. These features include: (1) multiple subtopics in a single document are allowed, which is close to reality; (2) the user's information need on a certain subtopic can be fulfilled after collecting enough data; (3) different subtopics may have different importance with respect to each query; and (4) an IR system is considered performing better if it allow users to spend less time to gain more information. The recent TREC Dynamic Domain Track used this metric for evaluating dynamic and interactive search systems.

6.1 IR EVALUATION

Most Information Retrieval (IR) evaluation measures only determine the effectiveness of an IR system for one-shot queries. However, search rarely happens independent of other queries. In White, Muresan and Marchionini's report on evaluating exploratory search systems [254], the authors pointed out measuring effectiveness of session-based search should be based on *interactive behavior, cognitive load* and *the understanding of the exploring user*. More recent work [130] also recognizes that a more comprehensive measure should evaluate an IR system over a session involving multiple queries. Sessions involve query reformulations as the user progresses toward their goal. Thus a Dynamic IR system should be evaluated on how well it provides results for the whole session rather than for isolated queries.

Due to the scope and complexity of the user's involvement in the task, evaluation for session search is often done subjectively through surveys and questionnaires [162, 181, 254]. However, subjective evaluations usually do not suit well for large scale evaluations; the evaluation results are difficult to reproduce, too. As an alternative, for decades, the IR research community has worked extensively on developing system-based IR evaluation metrics. However, most of the work has been focused on evaluating ad-hoc search, i.e., retrieving ranked documents for a single query. A key difference between session-based search and ad-hoc search is that the former consists of multiple iterations of searches that depend on each other, and the session develops as time goes by. Little is yet known on how to evaluate a search engine's effectiveness for the entire course using a system-based metric.

Recognizing the ineffectiveness of single query metrics for session-based IR evaluation, Järvelin et al. [115] extended the Discounted Cumulated Gain (DCG) into a new, session-based metric for handling multiple queries in a session. They formulated a session-based IR evaluation model with key attributes, including the exploratory nature of search, the lack of optimal nature in initial query formulation, unstable queries, the learning process of the user during a session, the desire for highly relevant documents, and variation in stopping points across search tasks and individuals. Under this metric, costs occur when a user examines retrieval results and when a user revisits the query. Session-based normalized DCG (snDCG) is the cumulative gain value ranging from the first retrieved document to the corresponding documents of interest. Note in snDCG the n is number of iterations, not the same as n in nDCG where the n means normalization over the ideal gains. However, snDCG requires a fixed number of query reformulations, which might be a strong assumption in session search. Yang and Lad [264] expand upon this work by modeling the expected utility for information distillation systems. They model probability of all possible browsing paths due to query reformulation. They measure utility according to relevance and novelty, defined by the user interaction history in a document distillation task. Although their metric was not developed for session search in particular, it shares the similar spirit of developing a single metric for an entire process. Kanoulas et al. [130] expand on these works with respect to multiple queries by allowing the possibility of early session abandonment. They proposed both model-free measures that make no assumption about the user's behavior over a session, and model-based measures with simple assumptions of user interactions. All three pieces of work [115, 130, 264] are founded upon the assumption that all reformulations are directed toward a single information need.

The complex information need when users use a Dynamic IR system often consists of multiple aspects. Evaluating subtopic relevance is thus an important part of Dynamic IR evaluation. The TREC 6 Interactive Track [147] used *aspectual recall* and *aspectual precision* to measure how well a system allows a user to find documents which supply multiple instances for an aspect. Note that *aspectual recall* and *aspectual precision* are of a similar spirit to later work on diversity and novelty measures for IR evaluation. These include [274]'s subtopic recall, subtopic precision and weighted subtopic precision; Clarke et al.'s α-nDCG [61] (used in the TREC Web Track [60] diversity task and the TREC Tasks Track [267]) expands on the notion of gain in DCG being a constant value to incorporate uncertainty, ambiguity and redundancy in retrieved results. These also include Sakai et al.'s nERR-IA [207] (used in TREC 2015 Tasks Track), which assumes that, given a query q with several different subtopics, the probability of each subtopic can be estimated based on a multinomial assumption. Other recent metrics that consider subtopic relevance including I-rec [205] and D-nDCG [207] are all quite similar to either α-nDCG or nERR-IA.

Moreover, time being taken by the search system to satisfy the user's needs is a crucial factor in measuring effectiveness of a Dynamic IR system. The Cube Test is one of the earliest works that incorporate time as a dimension into IR evaluation. Later studies such as [266] have confirmed that the utility of a document is directly influenced by the degree of effort required by a user to find the relevant information in that document; the effort of the user depends on the judging time and dwell time. We are aware of related work, although for the ad-hoc search tasks, when time has been taken into account. The time-based-gain measure (TBG) [230] models the time actually spent by taking into consideration factors such as document length, duplicate documents and whether a summary is read prior to clicking and reading a document. Smucker et al. [230] calibrated a function that estimates the time it takes the user to reach document rank k TBG $= \sum_{k=1}^{\infty} g_k \exp\left(-\text{Time}(k)\frac{\ln 2}{\text{halflife}}\right)$. TBG is one of a few system-based metrics that are actually able to model user behaviors, even while they might still be oversimplified versions of actual complex user behaviors in the real world.

When Dynamic IR systems are task-oriented, it is also important to model users' satisfaction levels in an evaluation metric developed for it. For instance, modeling a stopping criteria [166] by using a cap over the gains. This is related to another line of research about user frustration. Early work includes Feild et al.'s [81] which studied and predicted user frustration on web search. But the cause of the frustration or the type of frustration was not explained in the paper, and the model needs to be personalized for different users. The Cube Test, which we will look into later, as a single metric, models a user's loss of interest in a subtopic by introducing a stopping criterion for the subtopic. The user does not gain useful information after the stopping criterion has been reached, which makes the metric distinct from other metrics considering subtopic relevance.

6.2   TEXT RETRIEVAL CONFERENCE (TREC)

The Text REtrieval Conference (TREC) is the annual evaluation of IR systems conducted at the National Institute of Science and Technology (NIST) since 1992. "The TREC conferences encourage research within the information retrieval community by providing the infrastructure necessary for large-scale evaluation of text retrieval methodologies."[1] Tasks that involved multiple runs of search iterations have been studied multiple times in TREC. From 1997 to 2002, the TREC Interactive Track [147, 181] investigated interactive, session-based search tasks with a

---

[1]http://trec.nist.gov

human user in the loop. The Track used *aspectual recall* and *aspectual precision* to measure how well a system allows a user to find documents which supply multiple instances for an aspect. Survey-based user studies were also used in the evaluation. Since no separation of the user and the search engine was done in the evaluation, it is difficult to tell a search system's effectiveness in the task. From 2010 to 2014, the TREC Session Track [131–133] sought to evaluate search effectiveness for the last iteration of retrieval at the end of a session given query logs of all previous iterations. The Session Track used an effectiveness measure for ad-hoc retrieval, nDCG [113], as the main metric to only evaluate the last iteration. As a results, the Session Track measured effectiveness at the end of the session, instead of over a session's entire course.

In 2015, the TREC Dynamic Domain (DD) Track [260] revamped the interest of session-based search. By providing a real-time simulated user (called the "jig") interacting with a search system for a number of iterations until the search stops.[2] A new metric, the Cube Test [166], originally proposed by Luo et al. [166], was picked as the main metric in the Track. The Cube Test was created based on the "water filling" model,[3] which likens finding relevant information for multiple-faceted information needs through a session to "pouring document water into a segmented task cube." The Cube Test is a single metric but generally includes a wide range of features that characterize session-based search, including subtopic relevance, retrieval speed and stopping of the search.

6.2.1   TREC INTERACTIVE TRACK

The TREC Interactive Track ran from 1996 to 2002 [181]. This Track mandated a common experimental design that allowed some degree of comparability between user studies done by different participating TREC teams. In 1997 and 1998 (TRECs 6 and 7), the setup of the track-encoded system outputs as "runs" which we were able to reuse as search sessions.

Each Interactive Track team conducted a user study in which people used search systems to collect relevant information for topics provided by NIST. They also asked users to fill out a questionnaire at the end of each study. A standard starting query was run by all searchers and the time between pressing the search button and the return of the results was logged. This information was used to get some idea of the different response time conditions searchers may encounter. Usually, all human searchers were required to be given at least 10 minutes on each task once the actual searching began and participating groups reported the results at the end of the 10 minute period in their notebook papers. Groups optionally decided to report additional results, e.g., after 5 minutes, 15 minutes, etc.

The corpus used here is the *Financial Times* of London 1991–1994 collection. Table 6.1 includes its statistics for TREC 1997 and 1998 Interactive Tracks.

---

[2]The search system decides when to stop.
[3]The model was developed based on a two-week user study conducted at the U.S. Patent and Trademark Office in 2012. During the study, more than 30 patent examiners were interviewed and closely observed how they search.

Table 6.1: TREC datasets and task statistics

Dataset	#Docs	Size	Avg. Doc. Length	#Unique Terms	#Topics	$Subtopic Per Topic	Avg. #Subtopics Covered by a Rel. Doc.	Avg. Rel. Docs Per Subtopic	Avg. Rel. Docs Per Topic
DD Ebola	0.66 M	13 GB	0.95 K	1.1 M	40	5.7	1.3	136	603
DD Illicit Goods	0.47 M	8 GB	0.46 K	3.6 M	30	5.3	1.3	9	39
DD Local Politics	0.96 M	58 GB	1.21 K	1.1 M	48	5.5	1.6	42	141
Interactive '97	0.2 M	412 MB	0.4 K	0.2 M	6	15	18.28	70.9	58.2
Interactive '98	0.2 M	412 MB	0.4 K	0.2 M	8	18.5	19.13	101.7	98.4
Session '12	50 M	433 GB	0.8 K	87.3 M	48	1	1	372.1	372.1
Session '13	52 M	552 GB	0.76 K	163 M	49	1	1	268	268
Session '14	52 M	552 GB	0.76 K	163 M	51	1	1	332.3	332.3

Table 6.2: Submitted runs statistics

Dataset	Min. #Iterations	Max #Iterations	Avg. #Iterations	#Runs	#Docs Per Iteration
DD '15	1	792	115	32	5
Interactive '97	1	44	12	8	1
Interactive '98	1	24	9	10	1
Session '12	11	11	11	9	50
Session '13	21	21	21	9	50
Session '14	8	8	8	9	50

There are only a few search topics in the Interactive Track. The topics include "looking for personal health information," "seeking guidance on US government laws, regulations, guidelines, policy," "making travel plans," "gathering material for a report on a given subject," etc. The topics contain aspects, which we term "subtopics" in this paper. Table 6.3 shows one example topic.

Table 6.3: Topic 303i in TREC-6 (1997) interactive track

	Subtopics of "Hubble Telescope Achievements"
1	Has inspired new cosmological theories
2	Study of gravitational lenses
3	More precise estimate of scale, size, and age of universe
4	Picture of more distant galaxies/objects
5	Generally good, better, better than expected results
6	Contradicted existing cosmological theories
7	Supported existing cosmological theories

We run our experiments on the official submissions of TREC 1997 and 1998 Interactive Tracks. There were 8 submissions in 1997 and 10 in 1998 (Table 6.2). The average session lengths are 12 and 9, respectively.

6.2.2   TREC SESSION TRACK

The TREC Session Track ran from 2010 to 2014 [134]. The Track organizers provided search topics and subtopics to human users, and asked them to search those topics using the Yahoo! search engine. The session logs were recorded during the search. The logs contain users behavior data such as queries they wrote, the retrieval results they obtained from the search engine, clicks and time spent examining documents. Table 6.4 shows a search topic about travel from the 2012 Session Track [131] with description of the search topics, subtopics and queries in the session.

The search systems were given the log of these existing sessions from iteration 1 to iteration $(t - 1)$, and were asked to retrieve for the last query in the session, i.e., complete the last search iteration t. This task is not a real-time interactive search task, however it is still session-based. Due to the setting of this Track, the official submissions to the Session Tracks only contain the search results for the last iteration. As such, we do not have all the intermediate iteration results, which makes it difficult to evaluate the submissions with a session-based metric. However, we reimplemented a few submissions based on their published papers. The statistics of these runs can be found in Table 6.2. There are nine approaches being reimplemented, including variations of "lemur" [153], "qcm" [94], "winwin" [168], and the original retrieval results embedded in the TREC Session Track query logs.

The Session Track topics do not have subtopic relevance judgments. The three topic sets all have approximately fifty topics and 250–350 relevant documents per topic. Table 6.4 shows an example Session Track topic from 2012. The runs that we implemented search an average of 11 iterations per topic in the 2012 topics, 21 iterations in the 2013 topics, and 8 iterations in the 2014 topics. All runs that we implemented retrieved 50 documents in each iteration.

Table 6.4: Example topic from TREC 2012 session track

> *Topic: You are writing a summary article about the Pocono Mountains region. Find as many relevant articles as you can describing the region, things to see and do there (such as national parks, resorts, shopping, etc), and communities of people living there.*

6.2.3   TREC DYNAMIC DOMAIN (DD) TRACK

The Cube Test has been used as the main evaluation metric for the Text REtrieval Conference (TREC) Dynamic Domain Track [260] since 2015. The TREC Dynamic Domain (DD) track focuses on supporting research in dynamic, exploratory search within complex information domains. The Track provides passage-level graded judgments ranging from 1 (marginally relevant), 2 (relevant), 3 (highly relevant) to 4 (key result).

In 2015, the TREC DD Track [260] created a simplified model of the information seeking task. The task is described as follows. The participating systems receive an initial query for each topic, where the query is two to four words and additionally indicates the domain. In response to that query, systems may return up to five documents to the user. The simulated user responds by indicating which of the retrieved documents are relevant to their interests in the topic, and to which subtopic the document is relevant to. Additionally, the simulated user identifies passages from the relevant documents and assign the passages to the subtopics with a graded relevance rating. The system may then return another five documents for more feedback. The retrieval loop continues until the system decides to stop. All the interactions, aka, the multiple cycles of retrieval results, are used to evaluate a system's search effectiveness. An effective participating system is expected to be able to find the relevant documents as many as possible, using fewer runs of interactions. Figure 6.1 illustrates the task in TREC 2015 DD Track.

Thirty-two official submissions to the TREC 2015 DD Track are used in our experiments. Table 6.2 shows that the shortest session in DD runs only has 1 iteration, while the longest has 792 iterations. The average session length among all DD runs is 115.

Three different domains of data were used in the DD Track: (1) *Ebola*, a dataset about the Ebola outbreak in Africa and North America from 2014 to 2015. The dataset comprises 497,362 webpages, 19,834 PDFs, and 164,961 tweets. (2) *Illicit Goods*, a dataset of online posts from underground forums about how illicit and counterfeit goods such as fake Viagra are made, advertised, and sold on the Internet. (3) *Local Politics*, a dataset of web news items about regional politics in the Pacific Northwest, which is a subset of the TREC 2014 KBA Stream Corpus. The statistics of the DD datasets are included in Table 6.1.

The search topics were created by NIST assessors. There are 118 topics in the 2015 DD dataset, including 40 for Ebola, 30 for Illicit Goods, and 48 for Local Politics. In total, 58,758

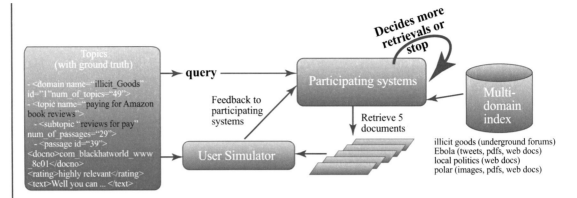

Figure 6.1: TREC dynamic domain task illustration.

Table 6.5: Example topic from TREC 2015 dynamic domain track

Topic	*CAPTCHA services*
1	**CAPTCHA service effectiveness**
2	CAPTCHA service names
3	**CAPTCHA hacks**
4	How to use CAPTCHA services
5	**CAPTCHA service costs**
6	CAPTCHA service descriptions

relevant passages were found and labeled by the assessors. These passages were used as the feedback data provided to the search systems.

6.3   THE WATER FILLING MODEL

In this section we present a conceptual user utility model called the **water filling** model. We propose that using a Dynamic IR system can be understood by an analogy of water filling a compartmentalized cube (see Figure 6.2). We also assume that searchers would like the multi-faceted components of the cube filled as quickly as possible. Based on this model a novel IR evaluation metric, the *Cube Test* (CT), is created, which:

- Covers different aspects or subtopics,

- Allows for a single document to cover several subtopics,

- Is time-sensitive, and

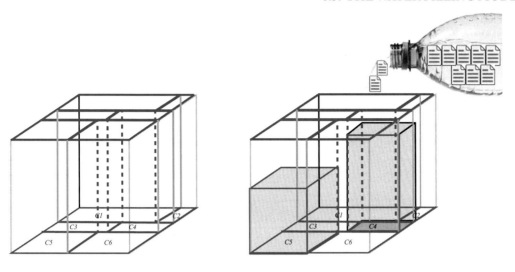

Figure 6.2: An empty task cube with 6 subtopics.

Figure 6.3: Filling "document water" into the task cube.

- Expresses the trade-off between time, quality of documents, and diverse coverage of subtopics.

We form an analogy between professional search and filling water into an empty container which we call a **task cube**. This model forms the basis of the *Cube Test* for evaluation.

Figure 6.2 shows the conceptual model of an empty task cube, which is intended to represent the user's overall information need. The task cube has unit length of 1. The segments of the bottom side of the cube represent subtopics, and the area of each segment represents the importance of the corresponding subtopic in view of the total information need. The area values are $\theta_1, \theta_2, \theta_3, \theta_4, \theta_5$, and θ_6 for subtopics c_1, c_2, c_3, c_4, c_5, and c_6, respectively. Each cuboid, or column, in the cube represents the information need of the corresponding subtopic.

We imagine each retrieved document as water that flows into all relevant cuboids. In some cases, there is a one-to-one mapping between returned documents and subtopics; and in other cases, a document's contents can flow into several different chambers of the cube if it is relevant to several different corresponding subtopics. The volume of water added to each cuboid varies depending on its relevance to the subtopic. By filling the cube with "document water," each cuboid contains water filled to various heights ranging from empty to full. As users examine documents they accumulate more information for the total need, but gaining information for each subtopic changes at different rates. Figure 6.3 shows this imaginary "water filling" process.

The height of the cube constrains the maximum amount of relevant information that a cuboid can contain, mirroring the maximum amount of relevant information that the user cares about for a given subtopic. Finding additional documents that map to a cuboid which is already filled cannot contribute more volume to the cuboid and does not provide any additional value to the overall information need of the user. Thus, once any cuboid of the task cube is filled, the corresponding subtopic need is considered satisfied.

The *water filling model* captures multiple dimensions in the general information seeking process. Recall-oriented IR problems prefer a set of documents that can contribute toward filling a greater number of cuboids, while precision-oriented IR problems prefer a few documents to produce high-volume cuboids quickly without requiring many cuboids to contribute.

The objective function of this water filling process is to fill up the entire cube with "document water" as quickly as possible. This equates to the goal of information seeking: to find enough relevant information as soon as possible. This intuition is used as the main optimization objective for the Cube Test to evaluate dynamic search systems.

6.4   THE CUBE TEST

The Cube Test [166] was designed based on the water filling utility model. By filling the cube with "document water," each cuboid contains water filled to various heights ranging from empty to full. As users examine documents they accumulate more information for the total need, but gaining information for each subtopic changes at different rates.

Calculation of the Cube Test simulates the water filling model for information seeking. The objective function of this water filling process is to fill up the entire cube with "document water" as quickly as possible. This equates to the goal of information seeking: to find enough relevant information as soon as possible. We can see that the Cube Test cares about both the amount of relevant information being received at the user's end as well as the time, or effort in general, spent to complete the entire task. It is therefore defined in the form of a speed function that is the rate of gain over effort or time.

Suppose we have an information need or a search topic Q, its subtopics c_i, where i is the number of subtopics in this topic, and D, a stream of incoming documents returned by a session search system. The documents arrive in batches (as those ranked in a SERP), iteration by iteration. Each iteration is indexed by t. Each batch is denoted by D_t with a batch size of b_t.

The *Cube Test* (CT) score for D, a stream of documents arriving in batches, to fulfill the task cube Q is:

$$CT(Q, D) = Gain(Q, D)/Time(D)$$
$$= \sum_{t=1,...,T} \frac{Gain(Q, D_t)}{Time(D)} \qquad (6.1)$$

where T is the total number of search iterations, D_t is the tth batch of documents returned by a system at the tth iteration, and $Time(D)$ is the time function to measure the effort spent in examining D, which will be discussed later. $Gain(Q, D) = \sum_j Gain(Q, d_j)$ and $Gain(Q, d_j)$ is the per-document gain for d_j.

When the batch size is reduced to 1, it derives a variation of the Cube Test, which is called Average Cube Test (ACT) that is also used in the TREC 2015 DD Track evaluation. ACT is equivalent to calculating the gain function at each document, instead of at the end of each iteration, then averaging the gains by the time function.

$$ACT(Q, D) = \frac{1}{|D|} \sum_{j=1,\dots,|D|} \frac{Gain(Q, D_{1,\dots,j})}{Time(D_{1,\dots,j})} \tag{6.2}$$

where $|D|$ is the total number of examined documents, $D_{1,\dots,j}$ is the set of documents examined by the user from the beginning up to the jth document. $Time(D_{1,\dots,j})$ is the time function to measure the effort spent in examining $D_{1,\dots,j}$.

Since Cube Test is an unbounded speed function, to put it in the range of $[0, 1]$, we normalize the raw CT or ACT values by an ideal maximum possible CT/ACT, which is calculated as the volume of the task cube divided by the smallest time unit. $Ideal\_CubeTest = MaxHeight * \sum_i \theta_i * max(Time^{-1}(D))$.

6.4.1   FILLING UP THE CUBE

The water filling model imagines each retrieved document as water that flows into all relevant cuboids. The height of the "document water" represents relevance and the volume represents gain.

Each document $d_j \in D$ being examined contributes some gain of information, mirroring the volume of relevant "document water" flowing into each subtopic in the task cube. The per-document gain $Gain(Q, d_j)$ is calculated as:

$$Gain(Q, d_j) = \sum_i area_i \, height_{i,j} \, KeepFilling_i \tag{6.3}$$

where i indexes the subtopics and j indexes the documents. $KeepFilling_i$ is an indicator function showing whether more "document water" is needed for subtopic i, which depends on the current amount of "document water" in that subtopic.

Mathematically, Eq. 6.3 is written as:

$$Gain(Q, d_j) = \sum_i \Gamma \theta_i rel(d_j, c_i) \mathcal{I} \left(\sum_{k=1}^{j-1} rel(d_k, c_i) < MaxHeight \right) \tag{6.4}$$

where $rel()$ is the relevance judgments between a document and a subtopic, which can be either binary or graded; θ_i weights the importance of subtopic c_i and $\sum_i \theta_i = 1$. $\mathcal{I}$ is the indicator function.

The Cube Test differs from existing gain metrics in two ways. First, it allows a document to be relevant to multiple subtopics, without necessitating a complicated ideal gain normalization. A one-to-one mapping between returned documents and subtopics is the trivial case. Second, the Gain function is not only a relevance score, but also incorporates relative subtopic importance. This framework supports more complicated notions of gain that relate to whole-task completion, critical insight, and/or relative gain tradeoffs between certain documents.

6.4.2 STOPPING CRITERIA

In Eq. 6.4, when d_j is under examination for subtopic c_i, if c_i has received enough evidence from previously examined documents (d_1 to d_{j-1}), d_j contributes nothing to c_i, which is captured by the indicator function: if the accumulated gain for concept c_i is equal to or more than *MaxHeight*, the maximum amount of relevance this subtopic needs, even if document d_j is very relevant to c_i, d_j's contribution is reduced to 0.

MaxHeight is a cap that the Cube Test uses to model the fact that in many real world session search tasks, such as patent examination or law enforcement, the search eventually stops. The reason for stopping a search is usually one of the following: (1) user's information need has been fulfilled, (2) the user is frustrated and the task ends, (3) or the user runs out of time or runs out of sources of information, i.e., the search results.

The cap of the task cube models the first point in the above list. Basically, finding additional documents that map to a cuboid which is already filled cannot contribute any additional value to the overall information need because the subordinate information need is considered satisfied.

The second point suggests modeling the amount of gain that a user actively acquires in the searching for a subtopic. A *monotonically decreasing function* is used to model a user's frustration as in MML in [81]: $rel(d_j, c_i) = rel(d_j, c_i) \times e^{a(-t)+b}$, where t is the iteration index, and a and b are smoothing parameters empirically set to $a = b = 1$. It suggests that a user needs more information at the beginning and less at the end of search.

6.5 PLOTTING THE DYNAMIC PROGRESS

Figures 6.4 and 6.5 plot the ACT and CT scores for all the runs submitted to TREC 2015 DD Track against the number of search iterations in the dynamic search process. The plots are averaged over all the 118 topics. The plots show a few things. First, they show how a run progresses as the number of iterations increases. In general all runs ACT and CT scores drop, which may indicate that later retrievals are harder so that the speed of getting relevant documents is harder. It may also suggest that how to best make use of the feedback becomes harder as the iterations develop. Noise could be introduced by extracting queries from the feedback messages. Not like in web search, where the user provides fresh queries constantly in a session, here the search engine needs to learn how to get the user's intent from the feedback passages, which could be limited if the search engine did not find any relevant documents at the earlier runs. Second, the systems use heuristics and criteria to mark the stopping points. From this year's graphs, we could not see where a good point to stop is partly because the relevance feedback from the first iteration was not sufficiently well used, thus the ACT and CT scores just drop after the first iteration. It looks like a challenge would be how to maintain a constant or even increasing speed of getting relevant documents.

We observe that ACT is slightly different from CT in that it might be a more stable metric; conceptually it is the average speed over every document being retrieved in the entire session. Thus, a system that is looking for a metric that is less sensitive to variation can look at ACT and apply it

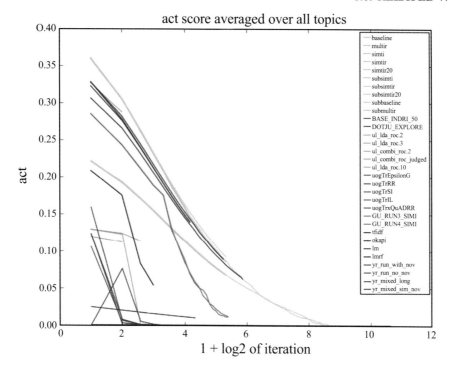

Figure 6.4: Average Cube Test (ACT) over the iterations (averaged for all TREC 2015 DD topics).

in the same manner as CT. The concaveness of ACT's metric curve would make it easy to identify a good stopping point for the ongoing search iterations.

We also plot all the ACT and CT curves for all runs on every topic. Due to the space limitation of this document, we only show ACT curves for two topics on which most teams score high and two other topics appear to be difficult to many teams. They are shown in Figures 6.6 and 6.7. Topic 36 is about searching for named entities, which could be easier for the systems. Topic 83 is on more general topics, which are more challenging for the systems. We observe that the systems are able to achieve high Cube Test scores at the beginning of a search process on the easy topics and then the speed of getting more relevant documents dramatically drops. On the difficult topics, the curves might be able to climb up when the iterations develop.

It is quite a challenge to evaluate a Dynamic IR system. We hope the metrics that we surveyed in this chapter could reveal the properties and capabilities of a dynamic system.

6.6   RELATED WORK

Widely used IR evaluation metrics emphasize evaluating ad-hoc retrieval. They include precision, notably MAP [199] and nDCG [114]. MAP measures precision by rewarding an earlier return

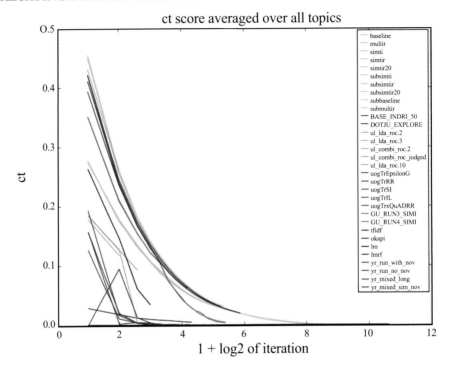

Figure 6.5: Cube Test (CT) over the iterations (averaged for all TREC 2015 DD topics).

of independently relevant documents. It assumes that relevance is binary and that the relevance of a document to a query is independent of the other documents previously returned [199]. NDCG [114] is an expansion upon discounted cumulative gain (DCG), which gives a higher score for documents with greater relevance that appear sooner in a ranked list. nDCG improved upon this by comparing this score to the ideal performance. Other IR evaluation metrics that also measure how early a system returns relevant documents, i.e., precision-oriented metrics, include GMAP [246], mean reciprocal rank (MRR) [18] and mean average generalized precision (MAgP) [7], [129]. GMAP uses a geometric mean instead of an arithmetic average as in MAP. MAgP is similar to MAP but is used in structured document retrieval. MRR is a useful evaluation when performing known-item queries. As [170] pointed out, these metrics would work well when the task is precision-oriented but might be insufficient when a task also depends on the recall of the system.

Evaluating Subtopic Relevance

Researchers have looked into evaluating subtopic relevance. Zhai et al. [274] introduce subtopic recall, subtopic precision, and weighted subtopic precision, which evaluate a search system's ability

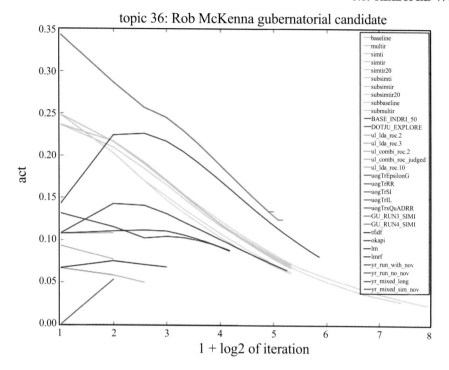

Figure 6.6: ACT for an easy topic (TREC 2015 DD Topic 36).

to return documents that cover subtopics of a general topic. The TREC 6 interactive track [147] used *aspectual recall* and *aspectual precision* to measure how well a system allows a user to find documents which supply multiple instances for an aspect.

The α-nDCG metric proposed by Clarke et al. [62] expands upon nDCG by incorporating α, the probability that the assessor made an error when judging whether or not a document is relevant. α-nDCG is derived from a probabilistic model. It models the probability that a document d matches to any subtopic c_i in the information need Q as

$$P(R = 1|d) = 1 - \prod_{i=1}^{m}(1 - P(c_i \in Q)P(c_i \in d)). \tag{6.5}$$

By making a few assumptions, the model simplifies to the gain function for the kth document in a ranked list:

$$\alpha\text{Gain@}k = \sum_{i=1}^{m} rel(d_k, c_i)(1 - \alpha)^{r_{c_i,k-1}} \tag{6.6}$$

where $rel(d_k, c_i) = 1$ if document d_k contains information for subtopic c_i, otherwise 0. $r_{i,k-1} = \sum_{j=1}^{k-1} rel(d_j, c_i)$ is the number of documents ranked up to position $k - 1$ that contains infor-

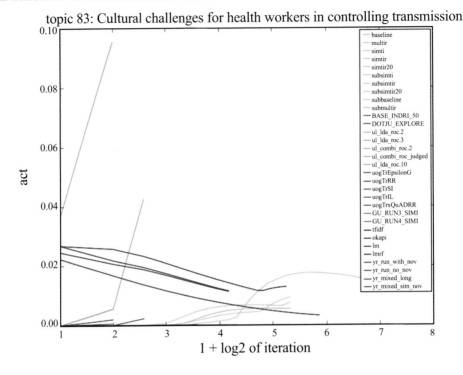

Figure 6.7: ACT for a difficult topic (TREC 2015 DD Topic 83).

mation for subtopic c_i. Notice that when $\alpha = 0$, α-nDCG reduces to standard nDCG with the number of matching subtopics used as the graded relevance value.

Other recent metrics that consider subtopic relevance include I-rec [205], nERR-IA [208], and D-nDCG [208]. *I-rec@k* is the percentage of matched subtopics at k and is defined as: $I\text{-}rec@k = \frac{|\bigcup_{j=1}^{k} I(d_j)|}{|C_q|}$, where C_q denotes the complete set of subtopics for a query Q, d_j denotes a document at rank j, and $C(d_j)$ denotes the set of subtopics to which d_r is relevant at the cut-off rank k.

nERR-IA [208] assumes that, given a query q with several different subtopics c_i, the probability of each subtopic $P(c_i|q)$ can be estimated and $\sum_i P(i|q) = 1$. It also assumes that document relevance assessments $rel(d, c_i)$ are available for each subtopic. nERR-IA is defined as:

$$\text{nERR-IA} = \sum_i P(c_i|q) \frac{\sum_{j=1}^{k} P(j) P_{\text{dis\_satisfy}}(j-1)}{\sum_{j=1}^{k} P^*(j) P^*_{\text{dis\_satisfy}}(j-1)} \tag{6.7}$$

where $P(j)$ denotes the relevance probability of a document at rank j. The probability that a user doesn't find the relevant document from document rank 1 to rank j-1 is $P_{\text{dis\_satisfy}}(j-1) =$

$\prod_{p=1}^{j-1}(1 - P(p))$. $P^*(j)$ is the relevance probability of a document at rank j in an ideal ranked list and $P^*_{dis\_satisfy}(j-1) = \prod_{p=1}^{j-1}(1 - P^*(p))$.

Similar to α-nDCG, D-nDCG [208] assumes that a document is relevant to a query if it is at least relevant to one subtopic. D-nDCG is calculated in the framework of nDCG, with the only change of introducing per subtopic relevance. Instead of a graded judgment for the whole query, D-nDCG uses a weighted combination of subtopic related relevance judgments as the global gain (GG):

$$GG(d) = \sum_i P(c_i|q)rel(d, c_i). \tag{6.8}$$

Both nERR-IA and D-nDCG employ $P(c_i|q)$, the probability of the ith subtopic for query q. $P(c_i|q)$ indicates the importance of the ith subtopic for the entire information need. The bigger $P(c_i|q)$ is, the more nERR-IA and D-nDCG favor systems that retrieve relevant documents for the ith subtopic. Saika et al. [208] estimated $P(i|q)$ uniformly or non-uniformly. The former assumes uniform distribution of subtopics, which is equivalent to nDCG. The latter estimates the ith subtopic probability as $2^{n-i+1}/\sum_{k=1}^n 2^k \approx 2^{-i}$ when n is reasonably large. Saika et al. reported that both approaches yield similar results.

Evaluating Efforts

When evaluating an IR system, regardless of whether the user's focus is precision- or recall-oriented, the time for the user to actually acquire information needs to be considered. Intuitively, documents ranked higher in the returned list save the user time. Käki et al. [125] created a measure termed *immediate accuracy* that represents how often users found at least one relevant result by the nth result selection. Another metric *search speed* measures the relevant answers obtained per minute. This has been modeled through metrics such as nDCG [114], Rank Biased Precision (RBP) [175], and Expected Reciprocal Rank (ERR) [53].

The recent time-based-gain measure [230] models a gain function that considers factors such as document length and duplicate documents. TBG models the time actually spent, rather than assuming a one-to-one relationship between document rank and time spent. The model considers whether a user spends more time reading a longer document, or if a summary is read prior to clicking and reading a document. The metric considers the time it takes the user to reach the position at which the document was ranked. Smucker et al. [230] calibrated their model based on a user study. According to their estimation, the time-based gain:

$$TBG = \sum_{k=1}^{\infty} g_k \exp\left(-\text{Time}(k)\frac{\ln 2}{\text{halflife}}\right) \tag{6.9}$$

where g_k is the gain of the kth document in the ranked result list, $g_k = 0.4928$ if the kth document is relevant, otherwise 0, and halflife=224 seconds. The expected time for a user to reach a document at rank k is: $\text{Time}(k) = \sum_{j=1}^{k-1} 4.4 + (0.018l_j + 7.8)P(C = 1|R = r_j)$, where l_j is the length of the document at rank j, r_j is the binary relevance judgment associated with d_j. $P(C = 1 | R = r_j)$ is the conditional probability that the user clicks the rth document given document relevance, set to 0.65 if $r_j = 1$, otherwise the probability is set to 0.39. TBG defines the time it takes the user to reach document rank k by keeping these variables constant with respect to time. In the Cube Test, the trade-off between search speed and the subtopic relevance is addressed and leaves for future work a calibration to more accurately model user behavior.

CHAPTER 7

Conclusion

In this book, dynamic information retrieval has been presented as a logical and necessary evolution of the current conceptual framework methodologies used in information retrieval research. Through the definition of a dynamic IR framework and related technologies in artificial intelligence and statistical modeling, links to existing areas of research have been established, including session search, online learning to rank and recommender systems. Further to this, consideration is given on how to evaluate dynamic IR problems. In summary, dynamic IR is a useful categorization of existing and ongoing areas of research in IR and, through the frameworks and methods described in this book, a useful platform upon which to build future research.

The Dynamic IR Framework In this book, dynamic IR was defined in the context of existing static and interactive frameworks in IR. This is an ongoing area of research building on the utility models proposed by Cooper in 1973 [66], where recent work has delved into the application of economic models to search, balancing the risk of costs vs. the benefits to a user of interactive ranking strategies [16, 17]. Further, the optimal setting of the components within these frameworks is an open area of research. In fact, the work in the later chapters can be considered as particular problem settings within this framework.

One of the essential models in dynamic IR is the Markov decision process. It is used in research throughout this book, in particular in session search, and it underpins the general dynamic IR framework. Typically when using Markovian solutions such as an MDP, a stationary solution can be found by taking the limit of the value function. This solution is usually easier to solve than by searching over the action and state space as is the case in value and policy iteration. Ultimately, the long-term objective for any problem solution in dynamic IR is to find a stationery solution to its dynamic model which can be applied in a practical, tractable algorithm. This solution would also give insight into the dynamics of the system itself and could be generalized to the dynamic IR framework itself.

Existing Dynamic IR Research An objective of this book has been to highlight key areas of existing research in dynamic IR, identify the core technologies used within that area, and to make clear the links to the dynamic IR conceptual model. Nonetheless, the coverage in this book is not exhaustive as there are many other areas of IR in which the principles that define a problem as dynamic can be applied. The work that has been reviewed in this book is that which has been chosen by the authors to represent the most prominent, current areas of the state-of-the-art in this exciting new area of research.

For instance, there has been a focus on research in session search in the previous 5 years, with the recent NSF task-based search workshop [137] providing a blueprint for a research road-map in the field, with a focus on incorporating models of tasks and user information needs into systems to support session search. Richer datasets combined with advances in query suggestion [233], auto-completion [223], contextual search [224] and user behavior modeling [117] all suggest that session search will be an important research topic for many years to come.

Online learning to rank, as well as the associated areas of adaptive filtering, relevance feedback and interactive retrieval are also continuing areas of research in IR. In particular, the profitability of recommender systems in advertising and e-commerce make this a field likely only to grow bigger and become more important over time. In support of this, multi-armed bandit theory and other reinforcement learning techniques are currently widely researched within the machine learning and artificial intelligence community, and it will be the application of these new techniques to dynamic problems in IR that will form the next range of research.

Evaluation in Dynamic IR   Ultimately, a key challenge facing the design of algorithms under the Dynamic IR framework is in their evaluation. While industrial practitioners in IR may have access to a live search system and users on which to perform A/B tests, these resources are not typically available to academics on a scale larger than expensive user studies. The inherent interactivity of Dynamic IR systems means that evaluating over offline test collections will always result in compromises. In recent years, some headway has been made in the use of offline datasets for the evaluation of online learning techniques [156, 158], in particular the work on causal inference which offers promising advances [186]. In addition, the recent TREC Dynamic Domain Track, TREC Open Search Track, and Living Labs for IR project allow academics to create document rankings for live users, a useful research tool for evaluating dynamic techniques. Some solutions, methodologies and evaluation metrics have been highlighted in this book although we concede that this is still a new and essential area of research for Dynamic IR.

Keep up to date with the latest in Dynamic Information Retrieval Modeling by visiting our websites `http://www.dynamic-ir-modeling.org/` and `http://infosense.cs.georgetown.edu/DynamicIR`.

Bibliography

[1] Eytan Adar, Jaime Teevan, Susan T. Dumais, and Jonathan L. Elsas. The web changes everything: Understanding the dynamics of web content. In *WSDM'09*, pages 282–291. ACM, 2009. DOI: 10.1145/1498759.1498837. 5

[2] Deepak Agarwal, Bee-Chung Chen, Pradheep Elango, and Xuanhui Wang. Click shaping to optimize multiple objectives. In *KDD'11*, pages 132–140. ACM, 2011. DOI: 10.1145/2020408.2020435. 5

[3] Deepak Agarwal, Bee chung Chen, Pradheep Elango, Nitin Motgi, Seung taek Park, Raghu Ramakrishnan, Scott Roy, and Joe Zachariah. Online models for content optimization. In *Advances in Neural Information Processing Systems 21*, pages 17–24. Curran Associates, Inc., 2009. 41

[4] Eugene Agichtein, Eric Brill, and Susan Dumais. Improving web search ranking by incorporating user behavior information. In *SIGIR'06*, pages 19–26. ACM, 2006. DOI: 10.1145/1148170.1148177. 35

[5] Rajeev Agrawal. Sample mean based index policies with O(log n) regret for the multi-armed bandit problem. *Advances in Applied Probability*, 27(4), pages 1054–1078, 1995. DOI: 10.2307/1427934. 39

[6] H. J. Ahn. A new similarity measure for collaborative filtering to alleviate the new user cold-starting problem. *Information Sciences*, 2008. DOI: 10.1016/j.ins.2007.07.024. 79

[7] M. S. Ali, Mariano P. Consens, Gabriella Kazai, and Mounia Lalmas. Structural relevance: a common basis for the evaluation of structured document retrieval. In *CIKM'08*. DOI: 10.1145/1458082.1458235. 94

[8] James Allan. Incremental relevance feedback for information filtering. In *SIGIR'96*, pages 270–278, 1996. DOI: 10.1145/243199.243274. 33

[9] Peter Auer. Using confidence bounds for exploitation-exploration trade-offs. In *The Journal of Machine Learning Research*, 2003. 77, 79, 80

[10] Peter Auer, Nicolò Cesa-Bianchi, and Paul Fischer. Finite-time analysis of the multiarmed bandit problem. *Machine Learning*, 2002. 80

[11] Peter Auer, Nicolò Cesa-Bianchi, Yoav Freund, and Robert E. Schapire. Gambling in a rigged casino: The adversarial multi-armed bandit problem. pages 322–331, 1995. DOI: 10.1109/sfcs.1995.492488. 40

[12] Peter Auer, Nicolò Cesa-Bianchi, and Paul Fischer. Finite-time analysis of the multiarmed bandit problem. *Machine Learning*, 47(2–3), pages 235–256, 2002. 25

[13] Peter Auer, Nicolò Cesa-Bianchi, and Paul Fischer. Finite-time analysis of the multiarmed bandit problem. *Machine Learning*, 47, pages 235–256, 2002. 39

[14] Peter Auer, Nicolò Cesa-Bianchi, Yoav Freund, and Robert E. Schapire. The nonstochastic multiarmed bandit problem. *SIAM J. Comput.*, 32(1), pages 48–77, 2002. Preliminary version in *36th IEEE FOCS*, 1995. DOI: 10.1137/s0097539701398375. 25

[15] Peter Auer, Nicolò Cesa-Bianchi, Yoav Freund, and Robert E. Schapire. The nonstochastic multiarmed bandit problem. *SIAM J. Comput.*, 32, pages 48–77, 2003. DOI: 10.1137/s0097539701398375. 40, 80

[16] Leif Azzopardi. The economics in interactive information retrieval. In *SIGIR'11*, pages 15–24. ACM, 2011. DOI: 10.1145/2009916.2009923. 99

[17] Leif Azzopardi. Modelling interaction with economic models of search. In *SIGIR'14*, pages 3–12. ACM, 2014. DOI: 10.1145/2600428.2609574. 99

[18] Leif Azzopardi, Maarten de Rijke, and Krisztian Balog. Building simulated queries for known-item topics: an analysis using six european languages. In *SIGIR'07*. DOI: 10.1145/1277741.1277820. 94

[19] Ashwinkumar Badanidiyuru, Robert Kleinberg, and Aleksandrs Slivkins. Bandits with knapsacks. In *54th IEEE FOCS*, 2013. DOI: 10.1109/focs.2013.30. 25

[20] Ricardo Baeza-Yates, Carlos Hurtado, and Marcelo Mendoza. Query recommendation using query logs in search engines. In *EDBT'04*, pages 588–596. Springer-Verlag, 2004. DOI: 10.1007/978-3-540-30192-9_58. 17

[21] Justin Basilico and Thomas Hofmann. Unifying collaborative and content-based filtering. In *Proc. of ICML*, 2004. DOI: 10.1145/1015330.1015394. 70

[22] Holger Bast and Ingmar Weber. Type less, find more: Fast autocompletion search with a succinct index. In *SIGIR'06*, pages 364–371. ACM, 2006. DOI: 10.1145/1148170.1148234. 17

[23] Nicholas J. Belkin and W. Bruce Croft. Information filtering and information retrieval: Two sides of the same coin? *Communications of the ACM*, 35(12), pages 29–38, 1992. DOI: 10.1145/138859.138861. 33

[24] Richard Bellman. *Dynamic Programming*. Princeton University Press, Princeton, NJ, first edition, 1957. DOI: 10.1126/science.153.3731.34. 23, 37

[25] Richard Bellman. A markovian decision process. *Indiana University Mathematics Journal*, 6, pages 679–684, 1957. DOI: 10.1512/iumj.1957.6.56038. 23

[26] Omar Besbes, Yonatan Gur, and Assaf Zeevi. Stochastic multi-armed-bandit problem with non-stationary rewards. In *Advances in Neural Information Processing Systems 27*, pages 199–207. Curran Associates, Inc., 2014. 40

[27] Robert M. Blumenthal and Ronald K. Getoor. *Markov Processes and Potential Theory*. Academic Press, NY, 1968. 22

[28] Kurt D. Bollacker, Steve Lawrence, and C. Lee Giles. Discovering relevant scientific literature on the web. *Intelligent Systems and their Applications, IEEE*, 15(2), pages 42–47, 2000. DOI: 10.1109/5254.850826. 33

[29] Christina Brandt, Thorsten Joachims, Yisong Yue, and Jacob Bank. Dynamic ranked retrieval. In *WSDM'11*, pages 247–256. ACM, 2011. DOI: 10.1145/1935826.1935872. 20

[30] Sergey Brin and Lawrence Page. The anatomy of a large-scale hypertextual web search engine. In *WWW'7*, pages 107–117. Elsevier Science Publishers B. V., 1998. 13

[31] Andrei Broder. A taxonomy of web search. In *SIGIR Forum*, 36(2), pages 3–10, 2002. DOI: 10.1145/792550.792552. 2, 7

[32] Sébastien Bubeck and Nicolo Cesa-Bianchi. Regret analysis of stochastic and nonstochastic multi-armed bandit problems. *Foundations and Trends in Machine Learning*, 5(1), pages 1–122, 2012. DOI: 10.1561/2200000024. 25

[33] Sébastien Bubeck, Rémi Munos, Gilles Stoltz, and Csaba Szepesvari. Online optimization in X-armed bandits. *Journal of Machine Learning Research (JMLR)*, 12, pages 1587–1627, 2011. 25

[34] Chris Buckley. Automatic query expansion using SMART : TREC-3. In *Proc. of the Third Text REtrieval Conference (TREC-3)*, pages 69–80. 17

[35] Christopher J. Burges, Robert Ragno, and Quoc V. Le. Learning to rank with nonsmooth cost functions. In *Advances in Neural Information Processing Systems 19*, pages 193–200. MIT Press, 2007. 13, 31

[36] Fei Cai, Honghui Chen, and Zhen Shu. Web document ranking via active learning and kernel principal component analysis. *International Journal of Modern Physics C*, 26(04), 1550041, 2015. DOI: 10.1142/s0129183115500412. 36

[37] Wenbin Cai, Muhan Zhang, and Ya Zhang. Active learning for ranking with sample density. *Information Retrieval Journal*, 18(2), pages 123–144, 2015. DOI: 10.1007/s10791-015-9250-6. 35

[38] Wenbin Cai, Muhan Zhang, and Ya Zhang. Active learning for web search ranking via noise injection. *ACM Trans. Web*, 9(1), pages 3:1–3:31, 2015. DOI: 10.1145/2697391. 35

[39] Guihong Cao, Jian-Yun Nie, Jianfeng Gao, and Stephen Robertson. Selecting good expansion terms for pseudo-relevance feedback. In *SIGIR'08*, pages 243–250, 2008. DOI: 10.1145/1390334.1390377. 16

[40] Huanhuan Cao, Daxin Jiang, Jian Pei, Qi He, Zhen Liao, Enhong Chen, and Hang Li. Context-aware query suggestion by mining click-through and session data. In *KDD'08*, pages 875–883. ACM, 2008. DOI: 10.1145/1401890.1401995. 5

[41] Jiannong Cao, Kwok Ming Chan, Geofffrey Yu-Kai Shea, and Minyi Guo. Location-aware information retrieval for mobile computing. In *Embedded and Ubiquitous Computing*, vol. 3207, pages 450–459. Springer Berlin Heidelberg, 2004. DOI: 10.1007/978-3-540-30121-9_43. 4

[42] Zhe Cao, Tao Qin, Tie-Yan Liu, Ming-Feng Tsai, and Hang Li. Learning to rank: From pairwise approach to listwise approach. In *ICML'07*, pages 129–136. ACM, 2007. DOI: 10.1145/1273496.1273513. 31

[43] David Carmel and Elad Yom-Tov. Estimating the query difficulty for information retrieval. *Synthesis Lectures on Information Concepts, Retrieval, and Services*, 2(1), pages 1–89, 2010. DOI: 10.2200/s00235ed1v01y201004icr015. 7

[44] Ben Carterette and Rosie Jones. Evaluating search engines by modeling the relationship between relevance and clicks. In *Advances in Neural Information Processing Systems 20*, pages 217–224. Curran Associates, Inc., 2008. 34

[45] Ben Carterette, Evangelos Kanoulas, and Emine Yilmaz. Simulating simple user behavior for system effectiveness evaluation. In *CIKM'11*. DOI: 10.1145/2063576.2063668. 65

[46] Marc-Allen Cartright, Ryen W. White, and Eric Horvitz. Intentions and attention in exploratory health search. In *SIGIR'11*. DOI: 10.1145/2009916.2009929. 45

[47] Marc-Allen Cartright, Ryen W. White, and Eric Horvitz. Intentions and attention in exploratory health search. In *SIGIR'11*, 2011. DOI: 10.1145/2009916.2009929. 43, 44

[48] Nicolò Cesa-Bianchi, Claudio Gentile, and Luca Zaniboni. Worst-case analysis of selective sampling for linear classification. *Journal of Machine Learning Research*, 7, pages 1205–1230, 2006. 36

[49] Kian Ming Adam Chai, Hai Leong Chieu, and Hwee Tou Ng. Bayesian online classifiers for text classification and filtering. In *SIGIR'02*, pages 97–104. ACM, 2002. DOI: 10.1145/564376.564395. 33

[50] Deepayan Chakrabarti, Ravi Kumar, Filip Radlinski, and Eli Upfal. Mortal multi-armed bandits. In *Neural Information Processing Systems*, pages 273–280, 2008. 40, 41

[51] Olivier Chapelle, Thorsten Joachims, Filip Radlinski, and Yisong Yue. Large-scale validation and analysis of interleaved search evaluation. *ACM Trans. Inf. Syst.*, 30(1), pages 6:1–6:41, 2012. DOI: 10.1145/2094072.2094078. 35

[52] Olivier Chapelle and Lihong Li. An empirical evaluation of thompson sampling. In *Neural Information Processing Systems (NIPS)*, 2011. 75, 80

[53] Olivier Chapelle, Donald Metlzer, Ya Zhang, and Pierre Grinspan. Expected reciprocal rank for graded relevance. In *CIKM'09*. DOI: 10.1145/1645953.1646033. 97

[54] Olivier Chapelle and Ya Zhang. A dynamic bayesian network click model for web search ranking. In *WWW'09*, pages 1–10. ACM, 2009. DOI: 10.1145/1526709.1526711. 35

[55] Harr Chen and David R. Karger. Less is more: Probabilistic models for retrieving fewer relevant documents. In *SIGIR'06*, pages 429–436. ACM, 2006. DOI: 10.1145/1148170.1148245. 15

[56] Lydia B. Chilton and Jaime Teevan. Addressing people's information needs directly in a web search result page. In *Proc. of the 20th International Conference on World Wide Web*, pages 27–36, 2011. DOI: 10.1145/1963405.1963413. 43

[57] Aleksandr Chuklin, Ilya Markov, and Maarten de Rijke. Click models for web search. *Synthesis Lectures on Information Concepts, Retrieval, and Services*, 7(3), pages 1–115, 2015. DOI: 10.2200/s00654ed1v01y201507icr043. 34

[58] Massimiliano Ciaramita, Vanessa Murdock, and Vassilis Plachouras. Online learning from click data for sponsored search. In *WWW'08*, pages 227–236. ACM, 2008. DOI: 10.1145/1367497.1367529. 31, 41

[59] Charles L. A. Clarke, Eugene Agichtein, Susan Dumais, and Ryen W. White. The influence of caption features on clickthrough patterns in web search. In *SIGIR'07*, pages 135–142. ACM, 2007. DOI: 10.1145/1277741.1277767. 34

[60] Charles L. A. Clarke, Nick Craswell, and Ellen M. Voorhees. Overview of the TREC 2012 web track. In *TREC'12*. 82

[61] Charles L. A. Clarke, Maheedhar Kolla, Gordon V. Cormack, Olga Vechtomova, Azin Ashkan, Stefan Büttcher, and Ian MacKinnon. Novelty and diversity in information retrieval evaluation. In *SIGIR'08*. DOI: 10.1145/1390334.1390446. 82

[62] Charles L. A. Clarke, Maheedhar Kolla, Gordon V. Cormack, Olga Vechtomova, Azin Ashkan, Stefan Büttcher, and Ian MacKinnon. Novelty and diversity in information retrieval evaluation. In *SIGIR'08*. DOI: 10.1145/1390334.1390446. 95

[63] Cyril W. Cleverdon and Michael Keen. Factors determining the performance of indexing systems. Aslib Cranfield Research Project, Cranfield, England, 1968. 6, 17

[64] David Cohn, Les Atlas, and Richard Ladner. Improving generalization with active learning. *Machine Learning*, 15(2), pages 201–221, 1994. DOI: 10.1007/bf00993277. 36

[65] William S. Cooper. *The Inadequacy of Probability of Usefulness as a Ranking Criterion for Retrieval System Output*. University of California, Berkeley, 1971. 15

[66] William S. Cooper. On selecting a measure of retrieval effectiveness. In *The Journal of the American Society for Information Science*, 24(2), pages 87–100, 1973. DOI: 10.1002/asi.4630240204. 99

[67] Thomas H. Cormen, Charles E. Leiserson, Ronald L. Rivest, and Clifford Stein. Greedy algorithms. *Introduction to Algorithms*, 2001. 80

[68] Mark Cramer, Mike Wertheim, and David Hardtke. Demonstration of improved search result relevancy using real-time implicit relevance feedback. In *Understanding the User—Workshop in Conjuction with SIGIR'09*. 36

[69] Nick Craswell, Onno Zoeter, Michael Taylor, and Bill Ramsey. An experimental comparison of click position-bias models. In *WSDM'08*, pages 87–94. ACM, 2008. DOI: 10.1145/1341531.1341545. 34

[70] Van Dang and Bruce W. Croft. Query reformulation using anchor text. In *WSDM'10*, pages 41–50. ACM, 2010. DOI: 10.1145/1718487.1718493. 17

[71] Varsha Dani, Thomas P. Hayes, and Sham M. Kakade. Stochastic linear optimization under bandit feedback. In *COLT*, 2008. 80

[72] B. Demir and L. Bruzzone. A novel active learning method in relevance feedback for content-based remote sensing image retrieval. *Geoscience and Remote Sensing, IEEE Transactions on*, 53(5), pages 2323–2334, 2015. DOI: 10.1109/tgrs.2014.2358804. 36

[73] Mukund Deshpande and George Karypis. Item-based top-N recommendation algorithms. *ACM Trans. Inf. Syst.*, 2004. DOI: 10.1145/963770.963776. 79

[74] Abdigani Diriye, Ryen White, Georg Buscher, and Susan Dumais. Leaving so soon?: Understanding and predicting web search abandonment rationales. In *CIKM'12*, pages 1025–1034, 2012. DOI: 10.1145/2396761.2398399. 1

[75] Joseph J. Distefano, Allen R. Stubberud, and Ivan J. Williams. *Schaum's Interactive Feedback and Control Systems*. McGraw-Hill, 1994. 8

[76] Anlei Dong, Yi Chang, Zhaohui Zheng, Gilad Mishne, Jing Bai, Ruiqiang Zhang, Karolina Buchner, Ciya Liao, and Fernando Diaz. Towards recency ranking in web search. In *WSDM'10*, pages 11–20. ACM, 2010. DOI: 10.1145/1718487.1718490. 5

[77] Pinar Donmez and Jaime G. Carbonell. Active sampling for rank learning via optimizing the area under the roc curve. In *ECIR'09*, pages 78–89. Springer-Verlag, 2009. DOI: 10.1007/978-3-642-00958-7_10. 36

[78] Miroslav Dudik, Daniel Hsu, Satyen Kale, Nikos Karampatziakis, John Langford, Lev Reyzin, and Tong Zhang. Efficient optimal learning for contextual bandits. In *Proc. of the 27th Conference on Uncertainty in Artificial Intelligence (UAI-11)*, 2011. 80

[79] Carsten Eickhoff, Kevyn Collins-Thompson, Paul N. Bennett, and Susan Dumais. Personalizing atypical web search sessions. In *WSDM'13*, pages 285–294, 2013. DOI: 10.1145/2433396.2433434. 4

[80] Henry Feild and James Allan. Task-aware query recommendation. In *SIGIR'13*, 2013. DOI: 10.1145/2484028.2484069. 65

[81] Henry A. Feild, James Allan, and Rosie Jones. Predicting searcher frustration. In *Proc. of the 33rd International ACM SIGIR Conference on Research and Development in Information Retrieval*, pages 34–41, New York, NY, 2010. DOI: 10.1145/1835449.1835458. 83, 92

[82] Dennis Fetterly, Mark Manasse, Marc Najork, and Janet Wiener. A large-scale study of the evolution of web pages. In *WWW'03*, pages 669–678. DOI: 10.1145/775152.775246. 5

[83] Sarah Filippi, Olivier Cappé, Aurélien Garivier, and Csaba Szepesvári. Parametric bandits: The generalized linear case. *Advances in Neural Information Processing Systems*, 2010. 78, 80

[84] Peter W. Foltz and Susan T. Dumais. Personalized information delivery: An analysis of information filtering methods. *Communications of the ACM*, 35(12), pages 51–60, 1992. DOI: 10.1145/138859.138866. 16, 33

[85] Steve Fox, Kuldeep Karnawat, Mark Mydland, Susan Dumais, and Thomas White. Evaluating implicit measures to improve web search. *ACM Transactions on Information Systems*. DOI: 10.1145/1059981.1059982. 44

[86] Steve Fox, Kuldeep Karnawat, Mark Mydland, Susan Dumais, and Thomas White. Evaluating implicit measures to improve web search. *ACM Transactions on Information Systems*, 23, pages 147–168, 2005. DOI: 10.1145/1059981.1059982. 16

[87] Norbert Fuhr. A probability ranking principle for interactive information retrieval. *Inf. Retr.*, 11(3), pages 251–265, 2008. DOI: 10.1007/s10791-008-9045-0. 19, 20

[88] John C. Gittins. Bandit processes and dynamic allocation indices. *Journal of the Royal Statistical Society Series B Methodological*, 41(2), pages 148–177, 1979. 38

[89] John Gittins, Kevin Glazebrook, and Richard Weber. *Multi-Armed Bandit Allocation Indices*. John Wiley & Sons, 2011. DOI: 10.1002/9780470980033. 25

[90] Jeremy Goecks and Jude Shavlik. Learning users' interests by unobtrusively observing their normal behavior. In *IUI'00*, pages 129–132. ACM, 2000. DOI: 10.1145/325737.325806. 16

[91] Nadav Golbandi, Yehuda Koren, and Ronny Lempel. Adaptive bootstrapping of recommender systems using decision trees. In *WSDM*, 2011. DOI: 10.1145/1935826.1935910. 79

[92] David Goldberg, David Nichols, Brian M. Oki, and Douglas Terry. Using collaborative filtering to weave an information tapestry. *Communications of the ACM*, 35(12), pages 61–70, 1992. DOI: 10.1145/138859.138867. 69

[93] Dongyi Guan, Hui Yang, and Nazli Goharian. Effective structured query formulation for session search. In *TREC'12*. 66

[94] Dongyi Guan, Sicong Zhang, and Hui Yang. Utilizing query change for session search. In *SIGIR'13*. DOI: 10.1145/2484028.2484055. 45, 86

[95] Dongyi Guan, Sicong Zhang, and Hui Yang. Utilizing query change for session search. In *SIGIR'13*, pages 453–462. ACM, 2013. DOI: 10.1145/2484028.2484055. 43, 44, 52, 53, 55, 61, 63, 64, 65

[96] Fan Guo, Chao Liu, Anitha Kannan, Tom Minka, Michael Taylor, Yi-Min Wang, and Christos Faloutsos. Click chain model in web search. In *WWW'09*, pages 11–20. ACM, 2009. DOI: 10.1145/1526709.1526712. 35

[97] Fan Guo, Chao Liu, and Yi Min Wang. Efficient multiple-click models in web search. In *WSDM'09*, pages 124–131. ACM, 2009. DOI: 10.1145/1498759.1498818. 34

[98] Uri Hanani, Bracha Shapira, and Peretz Shoval. Information filtering: Overview of issues, research and systems. *User Modeling and User-Adapted Interaction*, 11(3), pages 203–259, 2001. 5

[99] Abhay S. Harpale and Yiming Yang. Personalized active learning for collaborative filtering. In *SIGIR*, 2008. DOI: 10.1145/1390334.1390352. 79

[100] Yin He and Kuansan Wang. Inferring search behaviors using partially observable Markov model with duration (POMD). In *WSDM'11*, pages 415–424. ACM, 2011. DOI: 10.1145/1935826.1935891. 35

[101] Larry Heck. The conversational web. *Keynote Presentation, IEEE Workshop on Spoken Language Technology*, 2012. 6

[102] Matthias Hemmje. A 3D based user interface for information retrieval systems. In *Proc. of the IEEE Visualization'93 Workshop on Database Issues for Data Visualization*, pages 194–209. Springer-Verlag, 1993. DOI: 10.1007/bfb0021155. 20

[103] Jonathan L. Herlocker, Joseph A. Konstan, Al Borchers, and John Riedl. An algorithmic framework for performing collaborative filtering. In *SIGIR*, 1999. DOI: 10.1145/312624.312682. 70, 79

[104] William Hersh and Paul Over. TREC-8 interactive track report, 1999. DOI: 10.1145/344250.344251. 7

[105] William Hersh, Andrew Turpin, Susan Price, Benjamin Chan, Dale Kramer, Lynetta Sacherek, and Daniel Olson. Do batch and user evaluations give the same results? In *SIGIR'00*, pages 17–24. ACM, 2000. DOI: 10.1145/345508.345539. 6, 17

[106] Daniel S. Hirschberg. Algorithms for the longest common subsequence problem. *Journal of ACM*, 24(4), 1977. DOI: 10.1145/322033.322044. 62

[107] Katja Hofmann. *Fast and Reliable Online Learning to Rank for Information Retrieval*. Ph.D. thesis, University of Amsterdam, 2013. DOI: 10.1145/2568388.2568413. 4, 31, 41

[108] Katja Hofmann, Shimon Whiteson, and Maarten de Rijke. Balancing exploration and exploitation in learning to rank online. In *ECIR'11*, pages 251–263, 2011. DOI: 10.1007/978-3-642-20161-5_25. 31, 42, 52, 55

[109] Thomas Hofmann and Jan Puzicha. Latent class models for collaborative filtering. In *Proc. of IJCAI*, 1999. 75, 79

[110] Vidit Jain and Manik Varma. Learning to re-rank: query-dependent image re-ranking using click data. In *WWW'11*, pages 277–286. ACM, 2011. DOI: 10.1145/1963405.1963447. 35

[111] Tamas Jambor, Jun Wang, and Neal Lathia. Using control theory for stable and efficient recommender systems. In *WWW'12*, pages 11–20. ACM, 2012. DOI: 10.1145/2187836.2187839. 1

[112] Bernard J. Jansen and Amanda Spink. How are we searching the world wide web?: A comparison of nine search engine transaction logs. *Information Processing and Management*, 42(1), pages 248–263, 2006. DOI: 10.1016/j.ipm.2004.10.007. 11

[113] Kalervo Järvelin and Jaana Kekäläinen. Cumulated gain-based evaluation of IR techniques. *ACM Trans. Inf. Syst.*, 2002. DOI: 10.1145/582415.582418. 7, 84

[114] Kalervo Järvelin and Jaana Kekäläinen. Cumulated gain-based evaluation of IR techniques. *ACM Trans. Inf. Syst.*, 20(4), pages 422–446, 2002. DOI: 10.1145/582415.582418. 93, 94, 97

[115] Kalervo Järvelin, Susan L. Price, Lois M. L. Delcambre, and Marianne Lykke Nielsen. Discounted cumulated gain based evaluation of multiple-query IR sessions. In *ECIR'08*. DOI: 10.1007/978-3-540-78646-7_4. 82

[116] Jiepu Jiang and Daqing He. Different effects of click-through and past queries on whole-session search performance. In *TREC'13*. 66

[117] Jiepu Jiang, Daqing He, and James Allan. Searching, browsing, and clicking in a search session: Changes in user behavior by task and over time. In *SIGIR'14*, pages 607–616. ACM, 2014. DOI: 10.1145/2600428.2609633. 34, 100

[118] Jiepu Jiang, Daqing He, and Shuguang Han. PITT at TREC 2012 session track. In *TREC'12*. 47, 63, 66

[119] Rong Jin and Luo Si. A bayesian approach toward active learning for collaborative filtering. In *UAI*, 2004. 79

[120] Xiaoran Jin, Marc Sloan, and Jun Wang. Interactive exploratory search for multi page search results. In *WWW'13*, pages 655–666. DOI: 10.1145/2488388.2488446. 11, 21, 36, 52, 53, 55, 66

[121] Thorsten Joachims. Optimizing search engines using clickthrough data. In *KDD'02*, pages 133–142. ACM, 2002. DOI: 10.1145/775047.775067. 31

[122] Thorsten Joachims, Laura Granka, Bing Pan, Helene Hembrooke, Filip Radlinski, and Geri Gay. Evaluating the accuracy of implicit feedback from clicks and query reformulations in web search. *ACM Trans. Inf. Syst.*, 25(2), 2007. DOI: 10.1145/1229179.1229181. 34

[123] Leslie Pack Kaelbling, Michael L. Littman, and Anthony R. Cassandra. Planning and acting in partially observable stochastic domains. *Artificial Intelligence*, 101, pages 99–134, 1998. DOI: 10.1016/s0004-3702(98)00023-x. 25

[124] Leslie Pack Kaelbling, Michael L. Littman, and Anthony R. Cassandra. Planning and acting in partially observable stochastic domains. *Artificial Intelligence*, 101(1), pages 99–134, 1998. DOI: 10.1016/s0004-3702(98)00023-x. 48

[125] Mika Käki and Anne Aula. Controlling the complexity in comparing search user interfaces via user studies. *Information Processing and Management*, 44(1), pages 82–91, 2008. DOI: 10.1016/j.ipm.2007.02.006. 97

[126] Satyen Kale, Lev Reyzin, and Robert Schapire. Non-stochastic bandit slate problems. In *Advances in Neural Information Processing Systems 23*, pages 1045–1053. 2010. 40, 41

[127] Satyen Kale, Lev Reyzin, and Robert E. Schapire. Non-stochastic bandit slate problems. In *24th NIPS*, pages 1054–1062, 2010. 25

[128] Jaap Kamps, Marijn Koolen, and Andrew Trotman. Comparative analysis of clicks and judgments for IR evaluation. In *WSCD'09*, pages 80–87. ACM, 2009. DOI: 10.1145/1507509.1507522. 34

[129] Jaap Kamps, Jovan Pehcevski, Gabriella Kazai, Mounia Lalmas, and Stephen Robertson. Focused access to xml documents. Chapter INEX 2007 Evaluation Measures. 94

[130] Evangelos Kanoulas, Ben Carterette, Paul D. Clough, and Mark Sanderson. Evaluating multi-query sessions. In *SIGIR'11*. DOI: 10.1145/2009916.2010056. 81, 82

[131] Evangelos Kanoulas, Ben Carterette, Mark Hall, Paul Clough, and Mark Sanderson. Overview of the TREC 2012 session track. In *TREC'12*, 2012. 7, 43, 44, 56, 84, 86

[132] Evangelos Kanoulas, Ben Carterette, Mark Hall, Paul Clough, and Mark Sanderson. Overview of the TREC 2013 session track. In *TREC'13*, 2013. 2, 43, 44

[133] Evangelos Kanoulas, Ben Carterette, Mark Hall, Paul Clough, and Mark Sanderson. Overview of the TREC 2014 session track. In *TREC'14*, 2014. 7, 44, 84

[134] Evangelos Kanoulas, Ben Carterette, Mark Hall, Paul D. Clough, and Mark Sanderson. Overview of the TREC 2011 session track. In *TREC 2011*. 86

[135] Maryam Karimzadehgan and ChengXiang Zhai. A learning approach to optimizing exploration-exploitation tradeoff in relevance feedback. *Information Retrieval*, pages 1–24, 2012. DOI: 10.1007/s10791-012-9198-8. 39

[136] Jaana Kekäläinen and Kalervo Järvelin. Evaluating information retrieval systems under the challenges of interaction and multidimensional dynamic relevance. In *Proc. of the CoLIS 4 Conference*, pages 253–270, 2002. 7

[137] Diane Kelly, Jaime Arguello, and Robert Capra. NSF workshop on task-based information search systems. *SIGIR Forum*, 47(2), pages 116–127, 2013. DOI: 10.1145/2568388.2568407. 65, 100

[138] Diane Kelly and Jaime Teevan. Implicit feedback for inferring user preference: A bibliography. *SIGIR Forum*, 37(2), pages 18–28, 2003. DOI: 10.1145/959258.959260. 16

[139] Jin Young Kim, Mark Cramer, Jaime Teevan, and Dmitry Lagun. Understanding how people interact with web search results that change in real-time using implicit feedback. In *CIKM'13*, pages 2321–2326. ACM, 2013. DOI: 10.1145/2505515.2505663. 11, 36

[140] Youngho Kim, Ahmed Hassan, Ryen W. White, and Imed Zitouni. Modeling dwell time to predict click-level satisfaction. In *WSDM'14*, pages 193–202. ACM, 2014. DOI: 10.1145/2556195.2556220. 16

[141] Robert Kleinberg, Alexandru Niculescu-Mizil, and Yogeshwer Sharma. Regret bounds for sleeping experts and bandits. *Machine Learning*, 80(2–3), pages 245–272, 2010. DOI: 10.1007/s10994-010-5178-7. 40

[142] Robert Kleinberg, Aleksandrs Slivkins, and Eli Upfal. Multi-armed bandits in metric spaces. In *40th ACM STOC*, pages 681–690, 2008. DOI: 10.1145/1374376.1374475. 25

[143] Jürgen Koenemann and Nicholas J. Belkin. A case for interaction: a study of interactive information retrieval behavior and effectiveness. In *CHI'96*, pages 205–212. ACM, 1996. DOI: 10.1145/238386.238487. 20

[144] Yehuda Koren, Robert Bell, and Chris Volinsky. Matrix factorization techniques for recommender systems. *Computer*, 42(8), pages 30–37, 2009. DOI: 10.1109/mc.2009.263. 71, 79

[145] Alexander Kotov, Paul N. Bennett, Ryen W. White, Susan T. Dumais, and Jaime Teevan. Modeling and analysis of cross-session search tasks. In *SIGIR'11*, 2011. DOI: 10.1145/2009916.2009922. 65, 66

[146] Anagha Kulkarni, Jaime Teevan, Krysta M. Svore, and Susan T. Dumais. Understanding temporal query dynamics. In *WSDM'11*, pages 167–176. ACM, 2011. DOI: 10.1145/1935826.1935862. 5

[147] Eric Lagergren and Paul Over. Comparing interactive information retrieval systems across sites: the TREC-6 interactive track matrix experiment. In *SIGIR'98*. DOI: 10.1145/290941.290986. 7, 82, 83, 95

[148] Lifeng Lai, Hesham El Gamal, Hai Jiang, and H. Vincent Poor. Cognitive medium access: Exploration, exploitation and competition. *CoRR*, abs/0710.1385, 2007. DOI: 10.1109/tmc.2010.65. 40

[149] Tze L. Lai and Herbert Robbins. Asymptotically efficient adaptive allocation rules. *Advances in Applied Mathematics*, 6(1), pages 4–22, 1985. DOI: 10.1016/0196-8858(85)90002-8. 38

[150] John Langford and Tong Zhang. The epoch-greedy algorithm for contextual multi-armed bandits. *Advances in Neural Information Processing Systems*, 2007. 80

[151] John Langford and Tong Zhang. The epoch-greedy algorithm for multi-armed bandits with side information. In *Advances in Neural Information Processing Systems 20*, pages 817–824. Curran Associates, Inc., 2008. 40

[152] Carsten Lanquillon and Ingrid Renz. Adaptive information filtering: Detecting changes in text streams. In *CIKM'99*, pages 538–544. ACM, 1999. DOI: 10.1145/319950.320061. 35

[153] Lemur Search Engine. http://www.lemurproject.org/ 86

[154] Jure Leskovec, Lars Backstrom, and Jon Kleinberg. Meme-tracking and the dynamics of the news cycle. In *KDD'09*, pages 497–506. DOI: 10.1145/1557019.1557077. 5

[155] David D. Lewis and William A. Gale. A sequential algorithm for training text classifiers. In *SIGIR'94*, pages 3–12. Springer-Verlag New York, Inc., 1994. DOI: 10.1007/978-1-4471-2099-5_1. 36

[156] Lihong Li, Wei Chu, and John Langford. An unbiased, data-driven, offline evaluation method of contextual bandit algorithms. *CoRR*, abs/1003.5956, 2010. 100

[157] Lihong Li, Wei Chu, John Langford, and Robert E. Schapire. A contextual-bandit approach to personalized news article recommendation. In *WWW'10*, pages 661–670. DOI: 10.1145/1772690.1772758. 31, 41, 77, 80

[158] Lihong Li, Wei Chu, John Langford, and Xuanhui Wang. Unbiased offline evaluation of contextual-bandit-based news article recommendation algorithms. In *WSDM'11*, pages 297–306. ACM, 2011. DOI: 10.1145/1935826.1935878. 100

[159] Wei Li, Xuerui Wang, Ruofei Zhang, Ying Cui, Jianchang Mao, and Rong Jin. Exploitation and exploration in a performance based contextual advertising system. In *SIGKDD*, 2010. DOI: 10.1145/1835804.1835811. 80

[160] Wei Li, Xuerui Wang, Ruofei Zhang, Ying Cui, Jianchang Mao, and Rong Jin. Exploitation and exploration in a performance based contextual advertising system. In *KDD'10*, pages 27–36. ACM, 2010. DOI: 10.1145/1835804.1835811. 41

[161] Greg Linden, Brent Smith, and Jeremy York. Amazon.com recommendations: Item-to-item collaborative filtering. *IEEE Internet Computing*, pages 76–80, 2003. DOI: 10.1109/mic.2003.1167344. 70

[162] Jingjing Liu and Nicholas J. Belkin. Personalizing information retrieval for multi-session tasks: the roles of task stage and task type. In *SIGIR'10*, pages 26–33, 2010. DOI: 10.1002/asi.23160. 44, 51, 66, 82

[163] Tie-Yan Liu. Learning to rank for information retrieval. *Found. Trends Inf. Retr.*, 3(3), pages 225–331, 2009. DOI: 10.1561/1500000016. 6, 31

[164] Jiyun Luo, Xuchu Dong, and Hui Yang. Learning to reinforce search effectiveness. In *ICTIR'15*. DOI: 10.1145/2808194.2809468. 44, 49, 50

[165] Jiyun Luo, Xuchu Dong, and Hui Yang. Session search by direct policy learning. In *ICTIR'15*, pages 261–270, New York, ACM, 2015. DOI: 10.1145/2808194.2809461. 44

[166] Jiyun Luo, Christopher Wing, Hui Yang, and Marti Hearst. The water filling model and the cube test: Multi-dimensional evaluation for professional search. In *Proc. of the 22nd ACM International Conference on Information and Knowledge Management*, CIKM'13, pages 709–714, New York, ACM, 2013. DOI: 10.1145/2505515.2523648. 81, 83, 84, 90

[167] Jiyun Luo, Sicong Zhang, Xuchu Dong, and Hui Yang. Designing states, actions, and rewards for using POMDP in session search. In *Advances in Information Retrieval*, vol. 9022 of *Lecture Notes in Computer Science*, pages 526–537. Springer International Publishing, 2015. DOI: 10.1007/978-3-319-16354-3_58. 9, 55

[168] Jiyun Luo, Sicong Zhang, and Hui Yang. Win-win search: Dual-agent stochastic game in session search. In *SIGIR'14*. DOI: 10.1145/2600428.2609629. 86

[169] Jiyun Luo, Sicong Zhang, and Hui Yang. Win-win search: Dual-agent stochastic game in session search. In *SIGIR'14*, 2014. DOI: 10.1145/2600428.2609629. 21, 49, 51, 52, 53, 55, 61, 66, 67

[170] Walid Magdy and Gareth J. F. Jones. PRES: a score metric for evaluating recall-oriented information retrieval applications. In *SIGIR'10*. DOI: 10.1145/1835449.1835551. 94

[171] Tariq Mahmood and Francesco Ricci. Learning and adaptivity in interactive recommender systems. In *ICEC'07*, pages 75–84. ACM, 2007. DOI: 10.1145/1282100.1282114. 17

[172] Thomas W. Malone, Kenneth R. Grant, Franklyn A. Turbak, Stephen A. Brobst, and Michael D. Cohen. Intelligent information-sharing systems. *Communications of the ACM*, 30(5), pages 390–402, 1987. DOI: 10.1145/22899.22903. 32

[173] Andrey A. Markov. An example of statistical investigation of the text eugene onegin concerning the connection of samples in chains. *Science in Context*, 19, pages 591–600, 2006. DOI: 10.1017/s0269889706001074. 22

[174] Daniel M. McDonald and Hsinchun Chen. Summary in context: Searching versus browsing. *ACM Trans. Inf. Syst.*, 24(1), pages 111–141, 2006. DOI: 10.1145/1125857.1125861. 7

[175] Alistair Moffat and Justin Zobel. Rank-biased precision for measurement of retrieval effectiveness. *ACM Trans. Inf. Syst.*, 27(1), pages 2:1–2:27, 2008. DOI: 10.1145/1416950.1416952. 97

[176] Taesun Moon and Jason Baldridge. Part-of-speech tagging for middle English through alignment and projection of parallel diachronic texts. In *EMNLP-CoNLL*, pages 390–399. Association for Computational Linguistics, 2007. 5

[177] Taesup Moon, Lihong Li, Wei Chu, Ciya Liao, Zhaohui Zheng, and Yi Chang. Online learning for recency search ranking using real-time user feedback. In *CIKM'10*, pages 1501–1504. ACM, 2010. DOI: 10.1145/1871437.1871657. 41

[178] Masahiro Morita and Yoichi Shinoda. Information filtering based on user behavior analysis and best match text retrieval. In *SIGIR'94*, pages 272–281. Springer-Verlag New York, Inc., 1994. DOI: 10.1007/978-1-4471-2099-5_28. 16

[179] James R. Norris. *Markov Chains*. Cambridge University Press, Cambridge, 1998. DOI: 10.1017/cbo9780511810633. 21, 22

[180] Oliver M. O'Reilly. *Engineering Dynamics: A Primer*. Springer, 2001. DOI: 10.1115/1.1383672. 7

[181] Paul Over. TREC-7 interactive track report. In *TREC'98*. 7, 82, 83, 84

[182] Lawrence Page, Sergey Brin, Rajeev Motwani, and Terry Winograd. The PageRank citation ranking: Bringing order to the web. In *WWW'98*, pages 161–172. 13

[183] Sandeep Pandey, Deepak Agarwal, Deepayan Chakrabarti, and Vanja Josifovski. Bandits for taxonomies: A model-based approach. In *SDM*, 2007. DOI: 10.1137/1.9781611972771.20. 25

[184] Sandeep Pandey, Deepayan Chakrabarti, and Deepak Agarwal. Multi-armed bandit problems with dependent arms. In *ICML'07*, pages 721–728. ACM, 2007. DOI: 10.1145/1273496.1273587. 40

[185] Nish Parikh and Neel Sundaresan. Scalable and near real-time burst detection from ecommerce queries. In *KDD'08*, pages 972–980. DOI: 10.1145/1401890.1402006. 5

[186] Judea Pearl. Causal inference in statistics: An overview, 2009. DOI: 10.1214/09-ss057. 100

[187] Jay M. Ponte and W. Bruce Croft. A language modeling approach to information retrieval. In *SIGIR'98*. DOI: 10.1145/290941.291008. 11

[188] Filip Radlinski and Nick Craswell. Optimized interleaving for online retrieval evaluation. In *WSDM'13*, pages 245–254. DOI: 10.1145/2433396.2433429. 31, 42, 65

[189] Filip Radlinski, Robert Kleinberg, and Thorsten Joachims. Learning diverse rankings with multi-armed bandits. In *ICML'08*, pages 784–791. ACM, 2008. DOI: 10.1145/1390156.1390255. 5, 31, 41

[190] Filip Radlinski, Robert Kleinberg, and Thorsten Joachims. Learning diverse rankings with multi-armed bandits. In *25th ICML*, pages 784–791, 2008. DOI: 10.1145/1390156.1390255. 25

[191] Karthik Raman, Paul N. Bennett, and Kevyn Collins-Thompson. Toward whole-session relevance: Exploring intrinsic diversity in web search. In *SIGIR'13*, 2013. DOI: 10.1145/2484028.2484089. 65

[192] Karthik Raman, Thorsten Joachims, and Pannaga Shivaswamy. Structured learning of two-level dynamic rankings. In *CIKM'11*, pages 291–296. ACM, 2011. DOI: 10.1145/2063576.2063623. 20

[193] Al M. Rashid, Istvan Albert, Dan Cosley, Shyong K. Lam, Sean M. McNee, Joseph A. Konstan, and John Riedl. Getting to know you: learning new user preferences in recommender systems. In *IUI*, 2002. DOI: 10.1145/502716.502737. 79

[194] Al M. Rashid, George Karypis, and John Riedl. Learning preferences of new users in recommender systems: an information theoretic approach. *ACM SIGKDD Explorations Newsletter*, 2008. DOI: 10.1145/1540276.1540302. 79

[195] Herbert Robbins. Some aspects of the sequential design of experiments. *Bulletin of the American Mathematical Society*, 58(5), pages 527–535, 1952. DOI: 10.1090/s0002-9904-1952-09620-8. 38

[196] Stephen Robertson. The probabilistic relevance framework: BM25 and beyond. *Foundations and Trends in Information Retrieval*, 3(4), pages 333–389, 2009. DOI: 10.1561/1500000019. 6, 11

[197] Stephen Robertson and Ian Soboroff. The TREC 2002 filtering track report. In *The 11th Text Retrieval Conference, TREC 2002*, page 27–39. Gaithersburg, MD: NIST, 2003. 33

[198] Stephen E. Robertson. The probability ranking principle in IR. *Journal of Documentation*, 33(4), pages 294–304, 1977. DOI: 10.1108/eb026647. 6, 14

[199] Stephen E. Robertson. A new interpretation of average precision. In *SIGIR'08*. DOI: 10.1145/1390334.1390453. 93, 94

[200] Stephen E. Robertson and Stephen Walker. Threshold setting in adaptive filtering. *Journal of Documentation*, 56(3), pages 312–331, 2000. DOI: 10.1108/eum0000000007118. 32, 33, 35

[201] John Rocchio. *Relevance feedback in information retrieval*, pages 313–323. 1971. 9, 16, 17, 19

[202] Ian Ruthven. Re-examining the potential effectiveness of interactive query expansion. In *SIGIR'03*, pages 213–220. ACM, 2003. DOI: 10.1145/860435.860475. 20

[203] Ian Ruthven. Interactive information retrieval. *ARIST*, 42(1), pages 43–91, 2008. DOI: 10.1002/aris.2008.1440420109. 2, 7, 17

[204] Ian Ruthven and Mounia Lalmas. A survey on the use of relevance feedback for information access systems. *Knowl. Eng. Rev.*, 18, pages 95–145, 2003. DOI: 10.1017/s0269888903000638. 17, 34

[205] Tetsuya Sakai, Nick Craswell, Ruihua Song, Stephen Robertson, Zhicheng Dou, and Chin-Yew Lin. Simple evaluation metrics for diversified search results. In *EVIA'10*. 83, 96

[206] Tetsuya Sakai and Zhicheng Dou. Summaries, ranked retrieval and sessions: A unified framework for information access evaluation. In *SIGIR'13*, 2013. DOI: 10.1145/2484028.2484031. 65

[207] Tetsuya Sakai and Ruihua Song. Evaluating diversified search results using per-intent graded relevance. In *SIGIR'11*. DOI: 10.1145/2009916.2010055. 83

[208] Tetsuya Sakai and Ruihua Song. Evaluating diversified search results using per-intent graded relevance. In *SIGIR'11*. DOI: 10.1145/2009916.2010055. 96, 97

[209] Ruslan Salakhutdinov and Andriy Mnih. Probabilistic matrix factorization. *Advances in Neural Information Processing Systems*, 20, pages 1257–1264, 2008. 71, 72, 75

[210] Gerard Salton, A. Wong, and C. S. Yang. A vector space model for automatic indexing. *Communications of the ACM*, 18(11), pages 613–620, 1975. DOI: 10.1145/361219.361220. 12

[211] Gerard Salton and Chris Buckley. Improving retrieval performance by relevance feedback. *Journal of the American Society for Information Science*, 41, pages 288–297, 1990. DOI: 10.1002/(sici)1097-4571(199006)41:4%3C288::aid-asi8%3E3.0.co;2-h. 16

[212] Badrul M. Sarwar, George Karypis, Joseph A. Konstan, and John T. Riedl. Application of dimensionality reduction in recommender system—a case study. In *Proc. of ACM WebKDD Workshop*, ACM Press, 2000. 71

[213] Andrew I. Schein, Alexandrin Popescul, Lyle H. Ungar, and David M. Pennock. Methods and metrics for cold-start recommendations. In *SIGIR'02*, 2002. DOI: 10.1145/564376.564421. 79

[214] Falk Scholer, Diane Kelly, Wan-Ching Wu, Hanseul S. Lee, and William Webber. The effect of threshold priming and need for cognition on relevance calibration and assessment. In *SIGIR'13*, 2013. DOI: 10.1145/2484028.2484090. 65

[215] Anne Schuth, Harrie Oosterhuis, Shimon Whiteson, and Maarten de Rijke. Multileave gradient descent for fast online learning to rank. In *Proc. of the 9th ACM International Conference on Web Search and Data Mining*, WSDM'16, pages 457–466, New York, ACM, 2016. DOI: 10.1145/2835776.2835804. 42

[216] Young-Woo Seo and Byoung-Tak Zhang. A reinforcement learning agent for personalized information filtering. In *IUI'00*, pages 248–251. ACM, 2000. DOI: 10.1145/325737.325859. 41

[217] Burr Settles. Active learning literature survey. Computer Sciences Technical Report 1648, University of Wisconsin, Madison, 2009. 35

[218] Xuehua Shen, Bin Tan, and ChengXiang Zhai. Context-sensitive information retrieval using implicit feedback. In *SIGIR'05*, pages 43–50. ACM, 2005. DOI: 10.1145/1076034.1076045. 35

[219] Xuehua Shen, Bin Tan, and ChengXiang Zhai. Implicit user modeling for personalized search. In *CIKM'05*, pages 824–831. ACM, 2005. DOI: 10.1145/1099554.1099747. 20, 66

[220] Xuehua Shen and ChengXiang Zhai. Active feedback in ad hoc information retrieval. In *SIGIR'05*, pages 59–66. ACM, 2005. DOI: 10.1145/1076034.1076047. 36

[221] Pannaga Shivaswamy and Thorsten Joachims. Online structured prediction via coactive learning. *CoRR*, abs/1205.4213, 2012. 36

[222] Pannagadatta K. Shivaswamy and Thorsten Joachims. Online learning with preference feedback. *CoRR*, 2011. 41

[223] Milad Shokouhi. Learning to personalize query auto-completion. In *SIGIR'13*, pages 103–112. ACM, 2013. DOI: 10.1145/2484028.2484076. 5, 17, 100

[224] Milad Shokouhi, Marc Sloan, Paul N. Bennett, Kevyn Collins-Thompson, and Siranush Sarkizova. Query suggestion and data fusion in contextual disambiguation. In *WWW'15*, pages 971–980, 2015. DOI: 10.1145/2736277.2741646. 4, 100

[225] Aleksandrs Slivkins. Multi-armed bandits on implicit metric spaces. In *25th NIPS*, 2011. 25

[226] Marc Sloan and Jun Wang. Dynamical information retrieval modelling: a portfolio-armed bandit machine approach. In *WWW'12*, pages 603–604. ACM, 2012. DOI: 10.1145/2187980.2188148. 42, 54

[227] Marc Sloan and Jun Wang. Iterative expectation for multi period information retrieval. In *Workshop on Web Search Click Data*, WSCD'13, 2013. 42

[228] Marc Sloan and Jun Wang. Dynamic information retrieval: Theoretical framework and application. In *ICTIR'15*. ACM, 2015. DOI: 10.1145/2808194.2809457. 26

[229] Marc Sloan, Hui Yang, and Jun Wang. A term-based methodology for query reformulation understanding. *Information Retrieval Journal*, 18(2), pages 145–165, 2015. DOI: 10.1007/s10791-015-9251-5. 1, 2

[230] Mark D. Smucker and Charles L. A. Clarke. Time-based calibration of effectiveness measures. In *SIGIR'12*. DOI: 10.1145/2348283.2348300. 83, 97

[231] Edward J. Sondik. The optimal control of partially observable markov processes over the infinite horizon: Discounted cost. *Operations Research*, 26(2), pages 282–304, 1978. DOI: 10.1287/opre.26.2.282. 21

[232] Yang Song and Li-Wei He. Optimal rare query suggestion with implicit user feedback. In *WWW'10*, pages 901–910. DOI: 10.1145/1772690.1772782. 65

[233] Yang Song, Dengyong Zhou, and Li-wei He. Query suggestion by constructing term-transition graphs. In *WSDM'12*. DOI: 10.1145/2124295.2124339. 100

[234] Amanda Spink, Bernard J. Jansen, and Cenk H. Ozmultu. Use of query reformulation and relevance feedback by excite users. *Internet Research: Electronic Networking Applications and Policy*, 10(4), pages 317–328, 2000. DOI: 10.1108/10662240010342621. 16

[235] Amanda Spink, Minsoo Park, Bernard J. Jansen, and Jan Pedersen. Multitasking during web search sessions. *Information Processing & Management*, 42(1), pages 264–275, 2006. DOI: 10.1016/j.ipm.2004.10.004. 5

[236] Niranjan Srinivas, Andreas Krause, Sham Kakade, and Matthias Seeger. Gaussian process optimization in the bandit setting: no regret and experimental design. In *27th ICML*, pages 1015–1022, 2010. 25

[237] Robert J. Sternberg. *Handbook of Intelligence*. Cambridge University Press, 2000. DOI: 10.1017/cbo9780511807947. 8

[238] Kazunari Sugiyama, Kenji Hatano, and Masatoshi Yoshikawa. Adaptive web search based on user profile constructed without any effort from users. In *WWW'04*, pages 675–684. ACM, 2004. DOI: 10.1145/988672.988764. 20, 35

[239] Richard S. Sutton. Learning to predict by the methods of temporal differences. *Machine Learning*, 3(1), pages 9–44, 1988. DOI: 10.1007/bf00115009. 23

[240] Arthur R. Taylor, Colleen Cool, Nicholas J. Belkin, and William J. Amadio. Relationships between categories of relevance criteria and stage in task completion. *Information Processing and Management*, 43(4). DOI: 10.1016/j.ipm.2006.09.008. 51

[241] Howard E. Taylor and Samuel Karlin. *An Introduction to Stochastic Modeling*, 3rd ed. Academic Press, 1998. 21

[242] Jaime Teevan, Susan T. Dumais, and Daniel J. Liebling. To personalize or not to personalize: Modeling queries with variation in user intent. In *SIGIR'08*, pages 163–170, 2008. DOI: 10.1145/1390334.1390364. 43, 44, 45

[243] William R. Thompson. On the likelihood that one unknown probability exceeds another in view of the evidence of two samples. *Biometrika*, 25(3–4), pages 285–294, 1933. DOI: 10.2307/2332286. 25

[244] Aibo Tian and Matthew Lease. Active learning to maximize accuracy vs. effort in interactive information retrieval. In *SIGIR'11*, pages 145–154. ACM, 2011. DOI: 10.1145/2009916.2009939. 36

[245] Long Tran-Thanh, Archie Chapman, Alex Rogers, and Nicholas R. Jennings. Knapsack based optimal policies for budget-limited multi-armed bandits. In *26th AAAI*, pages 1134–1140, 2012. 25

[246] Ellen M. Voorhees. The trec robust retrieval track. *SIGIR Forum*, 39(1), 2005. DOI: 10.1145/1067268.1067272. 94

[247] Thomas J. Walsh, István Szita, Carlos Diuk, and Michael L. Littman. Exploring compact reinforcement-learning representations with linear regression. In *UAI*, 2009. 77

[248] Hongning Wang, Yang Song, Ming-Wei Chang, Xiaodong He, Ryen W. White, and Wei Chu. Learning to extract cross-session search tasks. In *WWW'13*, 2013. DOI: 10.1145/2488388.2488507. 65, 66

[249] Jun Wang, Arjen P. de Vries, and Marcel J. T. Reinders. Unifying user-based and item-based collaborative filtering approaches by similarity fusion. In *SIGIR*, 2006. DOI: 10.1145/1148170.1148257. 79

[250] Jun Wang and Jianhan Zhu. Portfolio theory of information retrieval. In *SIGIR'09*, pages 115–122. ACM, 2009. 14, 41

[251] Christopher John Cornish Hellaby Watkins. *Learning from Delayed Rewards*. Ph.D. thesis, King's College, Cambridge, 1989. 23

[252] Xing Wei and W. Bruce Croft. LDA-based document models for ad-hoc retrieval. In *SIGIR'06*, pages 178–185. DOI: 10.1145/1148170.1148204. 6, 13

[253] R.A. White, Ryen W. White, and Resa A. Roth. *Exploratory Search: Beyond the Query-Response Paradigm*. Synthesis Lectures on Information Concepts, Retrieval, and Services Series. Morgan & Claypool, 2009. DOI: 10.2200/s00174ed1v01y200901icr003. 1, 11

[254] Ryen W. White, Gheorghe Muresan, and Gary Marchionini. Report on the ACM SIGIR 2006 workshop on evaluating exploratory search systems. *SIGIR Forum*, 40(2), pages 52–60, 2006. DOI: 10.1145/1189702.1189711. 81, 82

[255] Ryen W. White and Ian Ruthven. A study of interface support mechanisms for interactive information retrieval. *The Journal of the American Society for Information Science and Technology*, 57(7), pages 933–948, 2006. DOI: 10.1002/asi.20365. 16, 20

[256] Ryen W. White, Ian Ruthven, and Joemon M. Jose. A Study of Factors Affecting the Utility of Implicit Relevance Feedback. pages 35–42. ACM Press, 2005. DOI: 10.1145/1076034.1076044. 16

[257] Werner Winiwarter, M. Hoefferer, and B. Knaus. Adaptive information extraction from online messages. *Intelligent Multimedia Information Retrieval Systems and Management*, 1994. 32

[258] Jinxi Xu and W. Bruce Croft. Query expansion using local and global document analysis. In *SIGIR'96*, pages 4–11. ACM, 1996. DOI: 10.1145/243199.243202. 16

[259] Zuobing Xu and Ram Akella. Active relevance feedback for difficult queries. In *CIKM'08*, pages 459–468. ACM, 2008. DOI: 10.1145/1458082.1458144. 36

[260] Hui Yang, John Frank, and Ian Soboroff. Overview of the TREC 2015 dynamic domain track. In *TREC'15*. 7, 84, 87

[261] Hui Yang, Marc Sloan, and Jun Wang. Dynamic information retrieval modeling. In *SIGIR'14*, pages 1290–1290. ACM, 2014. DOI: 10.1145/2600428.2602297. 44

[262] Hui Yang, Marc Sloan, and Jun Wang. Tutorial on dynamic information retrieval modeling. In *Proc. of the 8th International Conference on Web Search and Data Mining (WSDM 2015)*, 2015. DOI: 10.1145/2684822.2697038. 44

[263] Jaewon Yang and Jure Leskovec. Patterns of temporal variation in online media. In *WSDM'11*, pages 177–186. ACM, 2011. DOI: 10.1145/1935826.1935863. 5

[264] Yiming Yang and Abhimanyu Lad. Modeling expected utility of multi-session information distillation. In *ICTIR'09*. DOI: 10.1007/978-3-642-04417-5_15. 82

[265] Yiming Yang and Abhimanyu Lad. Modeling expected utility of multi-session information distillation. In *Advances in Information Retrieval Theory*, pages 164–175. Springer Berlin Heidelberg, 2009. DOI: 10.1007/978-3-642-04417-5_15. 27

[266] Emine Yilmaz, Manisha Verma, Nick Craswell, Filip Radlinski, and Peter Bailey. Relevance and effort: An analysis of document utility. In *CIKM'14*. DOI: 10.1145/2661829.2661953. 83

[267] Emine Yilmaz, Manisha Verma, Rishabh Mehrotra, Evangelos Kanoulas, Ben Carterette, and Nick Craswell. Overview of the TREC 2015 tasks track. In *TREC'15, to appear*. 83

[268] Hwanjo Yu. SVM selective sampling for ranking with application to data retrieval. In *KDD'05*, pages 354–363. ACM, 2005. DOI: 10.1145/1081870.1081911. 35

[269] Shuai Yuan and Jun Wang. Sequential selection of correlated ads by pomdps. In *CIKM'12*, pages 515–524. DOI: 10.1145/2396761.2396828. 1, 21

[270] Yisong Yue, Josef Broder, Robert Kleinberg, and Thorsten Joachims. The k-armed dueling bandits problem. *Journal of Computer and System Sciences*, 78(5), pages 1538–1556, 2012. Preliminary version in COLT 2009. DOI: 10.1016/j.jcss.2011.12.028. 25

[271] Yisong Yue, Josef Broder, Robert Kleinberg, and Thorsten Joachims. The k-armed dueling bandits problem. *The Journal of Computer and System Sciences*, 78(5), pages 1538–1556, 2012. DOI: 10.1016/j.jcss.2011.12.028. 41

[272] Yisong Yue and Thorsten Joachims. Interactively optimizing information retrieval systems as a dueling bandits problem. In *ICML'09*, pages 1201–1208, 2009. DOI: 10.1145/1553374.1553527. 41, 42

[273] Oren Zamir and Oren Etzioni. Grouper: a dynamic clustering interface to web search results. In *WWW'99*, pages 1361–1374. Elsevier North-Holland, Inc., 1999. DOI: 10.1016/s1389-1286(99)00054-7. 20

[274] Cheng Xiang Zhai, William W. Cohen, and John Lafferty. Beyond independent relevance: Methods and evaluation metrics for subtopic retrieval. In *SIGIR'03*, pages 10–17. ACM, 2003. DOI: 10.1145/2795403.2795405. 82, 94

[275] Lanbo Zhang and Yi Zhang. Interactive retrieval based on faceted feedback. In *SIGIR'10*, pages 363–370. ACM, 2010. DOI: 10.1145/1835449.1835511. 16, 17

[276] Sicong Zhang, Dongyi Guan, and Hui Yang. Query change as relevance feedback in session search. In *SIGIR'13*, pages 821–824. ACM, 2013. DOI: 10.1145/2484028.2484171. 65

[277] Sicong Zhang, Jiyun Luo, and Hui Yang. A pomdp model for content-free document re-ranking. In *Proc. of the 37th International ACM SIGIR Conference on Research and Development in Information Retrieval*, pages 1139–1142, 2014. DOI: 10.1145/2600428.2609529. 21, 52, 53, 55, 66

[278] Yi Zhang. Using bayesian priors to combine classifiers for adaptive filtering. In *SIGIR'04*, pages 345–352. ACM, 2004. DOI: 10.1145/1008992.1009052. 33

[279] Yi Zhang, Jamie Callan, and Thomas Minka. Novelty and redundancy detection in adaptive filtering. In *SIGIR'02*, pages 81–88, 2002. DOI: 10.1145/564376.564393. 33

[280] Yi Zhang, Wei Xu, and Jamie Callan. Exploration and exploitation in adaptive filtering based on Bayesian active learning. In *ICML'03*, pages 896–903, 2003. 35, 36

[281] Ke Zhou, Shuang-Hong Yang, and Hongyuan Zha. Functional matrix factorizations for cold-start recommendation. In *SIGIR*, 2011. DOI: 10.1145/2009916.2009961. 79

Authors' Biographies

GRACE HUI YANG

Grace Hui Yang is an Assistant Professor in the Department of Computer Science at Georgetown University. Grace's research interests include information retrieval, machine learning, natural language processing and text mining, with the current focus on dynamic search, search engine evaluation, and privacy-preserving information retrieval. Prior to this, she conducted research on question answering, ontology construction, near-duplicate detection, multimedia information retrieval, and opinion and sentiment detection. The results of her research have been published in SIGIR, CIKM, ACL, TREC, ECIR, ICTIR, and WWW since 2002. She was a recipient of the National Science Foundation Faculty Early Career Development (CAREER) Award. Grace co-organized the TREC Dynamic Domain Track and served as area chairs in SIGIR and ACL. She also served in the Information Retrieval Journal Editorial Board.
Homepage: http://www.cs.georgetown.edu/~huiyang

MARC SLOAN

Marc Sloan has completed a Ph.D. in Information Retrieval at University College London; his thesis was titled *Probabilistic Modeling in Dynamic Information Retrieval*. His research interests include applying reinforcement learning techniques such as multi-armed bandits and POMDPs to IR learning systems over time, contextual session search and query suggestion. Marc has published and presented IR research in top-tier conferences and journals such as WWW, SIGIR, WSDM, ICTIR and the Information Retrieval Journal. He has interned at Microsoft Research working on contextual, session based search result blending.
Homepage: http://mediafutures.cs.ucl.ac.uk/people/MarcSloan

JUN WANG

Jun Wang is a Reader in Computer Science, University College London, and the Founding Director of MSc Web Science and Big Data Analytics. His main research interests are in the areas of information retrieval, data mining and online advertising. He was a recipient of the Beyond Search award sponsored by Microsoft Research, US, in 2007; he also received the Best Doctoral Consortium award in ACM SIGIR06 for his work on collaborative filtering, the Best Paper Prizes in ECIR09 and ECIR12 for information retrieval, and the Best Paper Prize in ADKDD14 for computational advertising. He is also one of the recipients of Yahoo! FREP award 2014. He is an Area Chair of ACM SIGIR05 and has been a Senior PC member of ACM CIKM since 2012.

Homepage: `http://www.cs.ucl.ac.uk/staff/J.Wang`

Printed in the United States
by Baker & Taylor Publisher Services